Financial stewardship affects every area of ~
cle offers solid biblical advice for anyon‹
nances. In his new book, George Thomps‹
are on your financial journey and move t‹
through easy-to-understand terminology ‹ ... anecdotes. Whether
you want to eliminate debt or expand your savings, this book will help
you thrive in your finances.

ROBERT MORRIS

Founding Senior Pastor, Gateway Church

Bestselling Author of *The Blessed Life, Truly Free, and Frequency*

The Wealth Cycle addresses head-on some of the major issues that con-
front our society from a financial perspective today. For many years, I
have taught that the root of most financial problems is faulty thinking.
By candidly identifying some of the major faults in our thinking about
wealth, George helps us to see how we can reset our course toward financial health. Then, he lays out a process to manage cash flow and build
wealth. If you want to create a solid financial foundation for the future,
"Ready, Set, Grow" is a great place to start.

CHRIS GOULARD, CFP

Pastor of Financial and Benevolence Ministries, Saddleback Church

Chariman, Christian Stewardship Network

George has done an absolutely stellar job in bringing clarity to the complicated. Many people struggle to understand the economic divide. This
book is a refreshing guide to economic empowerment and those who
put into practice what George has captured here, will surely enjoy an
abundant life.

DEBORAH SMITH PEGUES, CPA/MBA

Bestselling Author of *30 Days to Taming Your Finances*

The Wealth Cycle, is a book that clearly illustrates the complexity of financial management in an easy to read, user-friendly manner. The book will not only show you how to get out of debt, but most importantly, how to accumulate wealth. In my 30 years in the real estate and financial industries , I have yet to come across a more comprehensive outline on building wealth that is universally applicable.

KEN LOMBARD
Real Estate Executive
Former President/Partner Magic Johnson Development Corp.

George's approach has power and clarity because it is simple and practical. I meet hundreds of people a year through my Coaching program and George stands out because he is always listening and learning. His focus and discipline shows through everything that he teaches.

MICHAEL P. GROSSMAN, CFP®
AdviceOne Empowerment Coaching LLC

Pastor George Thompson captures precisely how people of every walk of life can improve their personal financial outcomes. He has hit the nail on the head for building a blessed and meaningful life. He does it using a very big insightful and precise God inspired hammer.

STEVEN JOHNSON, CFO, FCBC
Pastor of Business & Finance (CFO), Faithful Central Bible Church

The Wealth Cycle

BUILDING A FINANCIAL LEGACY

George B. Thompson

The Wealth Cycle: Building a Financial Legacy
© 2016 George B. Thompson

ISBN: 0967485827
ISBN 13: 978-0967485829 (Prosperity Publishing)
Library of Congress Control Number: 2016944201
LCCN Imprint Name: Prosperity Publishing, Los Angeles, CA

The purpose of this book is to educate. Many facts set forth in this publication were
obtained from sources believed to be reliable, but cannot be guaranteed with respect to
accuracy. Any application of the investment or health advice herein is at the reader's
own discretion and risk. If additional financial or health assistance is required, seek
the advice of a financial or health professional. The author and the publisher shall
have neither liability nor responsibility to any person or entity with respect to loss,
damage, or injury caused or alleged to be caused directly or indirectly by the information
contained in this book.

All Scripture quotations, unless otherwise indicated, are taken from the Holy Bible, New
International Version®, NIV®. Copyright ©1973, 1978, 1984, 2011 by Biblica, Inc.™ Used by
permission of Zondervan. All rights reserved worldwide. www.zondervan.com The "NIV"
and "New International Version" are trademarks registered in the United States Patent
and Trademark Office by Biblica, Inc.™

Cover by: Vanessa Mendozzi
Layout and design by: Ljiljana Pavkov
Illustrations by: Phillip Taylor
Printed in the United States of America

George Thompson is available as a keynote speaker at conventions, seminars, and
workshops as well as for organizations. If you would like to discuss a possible speaking
engagement, send an email to inquiries@readysetgrowseries.com

For additional copies or bulk purchasing of this book, please contact:
Prosperity Publishing
P.O. Box 90761
Los Angeles, CA 90009
(800) 452-8001
www.georgebthompson.com

Contents

Figures

Tables

Time →
Talent → Jer. 29:11
Treasure →
Fasting →
   1. Put GOD First grow closer
   2.

Fin. Fasting
- Buy only things you need
- Use cash for all purchase. for next 21 days. No Debit/Credit
- No eating out, fast food, or dining.
- Prosperity Jar
- Journal - SOAP Scripture Observation Application Prayer

Spending Control →
Budget
Debt elimination
Savesting
Build Wealth

Pay the min all cards
except one
Debt multi $100.00

Do GOOD → Get out of
Debt

833 321 3222
www.george.b Thompson.com

Very Good Marketing
Operations
New Product
Dash board fin.

Real Estate

Acknowledgements

My goal for the Ready, Set, Grow series is to inspire you to change your thought process and ignite a fire in you to follow the Wealth Cycle - so that you can ultimately create the financial future that sets you free of the bondage of debt and worry. It's not enough to just change your mindset - actions must follow that change of mind, so you can be the best manager of what God has blessed you with. Over the last 20 years of teaching stewardship it has been a blessing to hear how the principles and tools that people have learned from my teachings have impacted their lives in a positive way. It is a humbling experience to hear and have so many people share their triumphs, their defeats and most of all their testimonies of continued growth.

My prayer is that your dreams get bigger and that your goals drive you even further. I encourage you to stretch and grow using the tools and principals in this series.

I am very fortunate to have so many people to thank. The following list is by no means complete, but first things first, I want to thank God! God makes all things possible and I am very grateful that I can wake up every day with a sense of purpose, knowing that I have been granted the opportunity to do what I love, sharing with others and helping them steward their time, talent and treasure. It is such a blessing!

Next, I would like to thank my loving wife, Kimberly who is walking on this journey with me. She is my heart and my balance. My three children, George, Alexander and Grace, are my personal motivation to grind even harder - you guys just make me want to do better and get better everyday. The greatest parents in the world George B. Thompson Sr. and Morsie L. Thompson(whom I miss dearly). They have both always loved and supported me, even in my craziest endeavors. (Yes, I have had some crazy ones.) My twin sister Jenifer, who has been the best sister a brother could ever ask for and my older brother Darrell who taught me many of the life lessons I carry with me to this day.

I would also like to thank Bishop Kenneth C. Ulmer whom I have had the pleasure of pastoring under at Faithful Central Bible Church as the Pastor of Stewardship and Finance. You have entrusted me with a responsibility that I have not taken lightly. The bible scholar I see in you has encouraged me to delve into the word of God even deeper and for this I am so very grateful. You are truly my mentor.

Dr. Kenneth Hammonds, I thank you for your mentorship and sharing of your wisdom and knowledge. I have grown to be a better husband, father and man of God due to our relationship. Thank you would never suffice - I have nothing but the deepest gratitude to you for your time, energy and efforts to pour into me.

This series is a culmination of all the dedicated contributions, hard work and energy of so many that have contributed to this project from inception to birth. Dannete Wilkerson for the years of hard work, insight and putting feet to vision - I sincerely thank you. Micah McKinney for putting in work. Thomas Z Lukoma and your wife for all the early morning meetings - for being the best editor in the world. Man, thank you for real. Faithful Central Stewardship Leaders, all MIT certified trainers , and Thompson Wealth Management - the TWM Crew.

Most importantly, I would like to thank the thousands of people that have allowed me to share my vision by participating in my seminars and attending my speaking engagements. Without your feedback, questions and personal sharing this series would not be possible. If you see any area of opportunity for improvement in the series please feel free to contact me because this book is for YOU!

Foreword

I'm constantly amazed at the volume and variety of titles in a bookstore. I often find some strange therapeutic benefit in casually navigating the aisles of the large bookstore near my home and marveling at the truth that if you "need it, want to know about it, how to do it, how to have it and what to do with it"- for the most part someone thought of it, addressed it, said it, codified it and wrote about it before your interest was even piqued! There is a book on just about any topic you can imagine.

To some degree I acknowledge that each book implies that each author has something significant to say, but I often conclude like the great musical "prophet" James Brown that many are "talking loud and saying nothing'." However, every now and then there emerges a fresh new voice with something to say that needs to be said and needs to be heard.

George Thompson is one such voice - one that speaks just as clearly to individuals who are struggling economically as to those who are of high net worth.

Thompson has a call on his life and a word in his heart that addresses his audience's view of prosperity to transcend the topic of money and address the principle of "Stewardship". Prosperity is therefore expanded to include all the gifts and talents bestowed upon an individual by their Creator.

Prosperity, health and deliverance are all in this work. In his series 'Ready, Set, Grow', he plots a path for his readers on how to experience a truly 'full' life through the correct stewardship of their financial resources - and the right mindset to be successful in all other areas of their lives.

The Wealth Cycle is the first book in this series and provides a practical journey into financial prosperity, financial health and financial deliverance - but is more than just that. It is a journey into a view of the world that starts with the premise that everyone has "greatness" within them; everyone was born to be a Champion. All they have to do is activate their purpose through purposeful stewardship. Profound but not preachy. Practical but not simplistic. Principled but not legalistic. This book can change your mind and your mentality about money and what it means to build wealth and a financial legacy.

Thompson's unique balance of biblical principles and practical application converge in a fresh approach and insightful implementation of the concept of Stewardship. Yet his passion for people beyond principles results in an exciting and challenging work that demands the reader to take a proactive posture of self-determination.

George Thompson has been sent by God to help you become all that God has ordained as a citizen and steward of the Kingdom. He will show you how to become a channel of blessings and not a reservoir of materialism. He will show you how to "be" more and not just "get" more.

Prepare to be motivated. Prepare to be challenged. Prepare to be blessed.

Bishop Kenneth C. Ulmer D.Min, Ph.D.

Introduction

Early in life, I recognized the disproportionate distribution of wealth in our country and its ever-widening gap. It troubled me to think about how the average person did not benefit from a financially viable economy that appeared to be enjoyed by only a select few. What principles did those who ascended into affluence use? How were their fortunes amassed? What basic factors created an environment of prosperity? What characteristics facilitated the preservation of that wealth?

And why did some people profit from economic environments successfully while others failed to thrive? For example, only a subset of the population took advantage of the booming stock market in the 1990s even though several opportunities were open to everyday investors and not just to professionals. On the other hand, when real estate was booming in the early 2000s, creating another

advantageous economic environment, thousands of people who got into the market then ended up in a worse place financially than they were before.

Finally, with so many scriptures in the Bible about wealth—such as John 10:10, which states: "I come that they might have life, and that they might have it more abundantly"—why did so many Christians suffer financially?

The difference lies in the money principles that guided their decisions. The problem is that these principles are not laid out plainly for everybody to learn. Yes, there are more books, blogs, podcasts, and television shows about personal finance than you could possibly consume in a lifetime, but just because information is available does not mean that it is accessible to everybody. Some people figure it out from these sources, but others consume the same information (or are aware of it) but never manage to climb out of their meager financial existence.

To unveil the mystery of this dilemma, I began to study how consistently wealthy individuals obtained and, more importantly, maintained their wealth. After several years of study, I learned some interesting principles. The most astounding of these was the tradition within our society of establishing generations of debtors.

We owe everyone.

There are bumper stickers that say, "I owe, I owe, it's off to work I go," reinforcing our accepted practice of robbing Peter to pay Paul. Being in debt is a socially accepted phenomenon, and we even have a politically correct way of tracking how much debt we have with the national system of credit history. Having a high credit score is a source of pride for many even though this does not necessarily mean you are good at building or maintaining wealth; all it means is that you are a very good borrower. And borrowing is not the true path to sustained wealth building; at some point you need to operate from the power of your assets, not your ability to obtain liabilities.

When your life is dictated by debt, you do not control your own destiny. To truly build wealth, you have to relieve yourself from the burdens of debt.

As I continued my investigation into wealth building, I discovered that not all millionaires obtain wealth in an underhanded manner, as is the common myth. In fact, the principles that are common among millionaires have more to do with living a life void of impulsive spending and having the ability to take ownership of their own future. During severe times, they seem to thrive, rather than withdraw, because of their moneymaking intelligence and unwavering discipline. They are not controlled by popular opinion. They do not act in fear, nor do they react to trends or fads. They remain focused.

I believe that the same capability to build wealth is available to all of us, if we apply the right principles to our own circumstances. Both sides of the coin, debt and wealth building, are an outcome of the principles that govern our financial lives and the actions we take because of those principles. Therefore, if we can learn the right principles and how to build the right habits to support those principles, we can be successful.

Armed with a keen understanding of these principles, I took it upon myself to outline the fundamentals in a language that anyone could comprehend. I began to donate my time to teaching classes at the beginner level. I found that most people are generally eager to learn about finances and how to accumulate wealth. The class, Reset: The Recovery, began to change lives. The feedback I received was so encouraging it began to enhance the quality of my own life. Some students could retire two years earlier, others could send their children to college, and others could live debt-free; the success stories were endless. The more I observed the phenomenal changes, the more I developed my sense of commitment to help people create and grow wealth.

This book is not my first, but it is different from my three previous books, *Millionaire in Training*, *The Total Package*, and *Set-4-Life*. In them, I covered similar subjects separately, but it was through my experience writing those books and teaching and training people that I realized how important it is to take a holistic approach to helping people improve their financial situation and thrive. Most people believe the financial world is a highly evolved and difficult field of study when in fact it is not. But no one I knew wanted to take the time to relay this information to those most in need. Rather than discuss money in isolation from the rest of their lives, I realized that to help people with their money, I had to help them be successful in all areas.

I wrote the Ready, Set, Grow series (*The Wealth Cycle* and *Set-4-Life: The Mindset of a Champion*) to provide a blueprint that you can implement at whatever stage of your financial life you are in to change your life and set you on the road to success. For those who are sinking financially, the series will help you to reset. If you are in a more stable financial situation, the series will help you to accelerate your results and grow. There is no particular order in which you should read the two books; just read them both.

In this book of the series, *The Wealth Cycle*, I will guide you through understanding how money works: both debt and wealth accumulation. I will provide you with the necessary tools to be successful while helping you to develop your own keen understanding of the fundamental financial principles that lead to sustained wealth building.

In order for this blueprint to work, you must follow each principle presented. You must make a commitment to your financial future, and you must be willing to change your mind regarding your finances.

Make the commitment to yourself and your financial future by signing the following contract with yourself.

My Financial Commitment

I, ..., promise and declare my commitment to be a good steward over my finances and every aspect of my life, including my time, talent, treasure, and family, and all that I possess. I will take control of my financial destiny and become wise and disciplined in my wealth-building habits. I will write down my goals and keep myself accountable to them. To do so, I will create a monthly spending plan, track my spending, and find extra money to pay down debt. I will invest in my financial education by buying books, attending seminars, and putting the principles I learn into action. I will get financial advice from a financial advisor as needed. I will never invest in something that I do not know anything about. I will communicate freely with my family about my finances and educate my children about business and finance.

I will set generational financial priorities and ensure that my wealth is passed on to future generations. I am committed to this declaration and will put into action all the knowledge I have obtained by reading this book and taking advantage of the tools that I have acquired through this financial learning journey.

By doing so, I will be set apart to build wealth for myself, my family, and future generations.

You are now on your way to financial freedom.

Chapter 1: # Wealth Building Is Stewardship

COMMAND THOSE WHO ARE RICH IN THIS PRESENT WORLD NOT
TO BE ARROGANT NOR TO PUT THEIR HOPE IN WEALTH, WHICH
IS SO UNCERTAIN, BUT TO PUT THEIR HOPE IN GOD, WHO
RICHLY PROVIDES US WITH EVERYTHING FOR OUR ENJOYMENT.
—1 Timothy 6:17

DO YOU NOT KNOW THAT GOD ENTRUSTED YOU WITH THAT
MONEY (ALL ABOVE WHAT BUYS NECESSITIES FOR YOUR
FAMILIES) TO FEED THE HUNGRY, TO CLOTHE THE NAKED, TO
HELP THE STRANGER, THE WIDOW, THE FATHERLESS; AND,
INDEED, AS FAR AS IT WILL GO, TO RELIEVE THE WANTS OF ALL
MANKIND? HOW CAN YOU, HOW DARE YOU, DEFRAUD THE
LORD, BY APPLYING IT TO ANY OTHER PURPOSE?
—John Wesley

Reading a book about wealth and building a financial legacy can conjure up all sorts of images in your mind—especially depending on your prior experiences. For some people, wealth is something that they fear because in the past they have seen wealthy people as their oppressors. They think wealth building is the same thing as becoming an oppressor themselves, so they subconsciously reject the idea, even if they may say something different.

For others, wealth is a goal that is attainable only for a select few—a group they don't see themselves joining. This is often because they have never been around wealthy people or have never had access to the tools or knowledge of how to achieve it.

Then there is another group that sees wealth building as purely evil. This became a popular narrative after the 2008 stock market meltdown because of the unethical and illegal behavior of several people that were seen as the select few (the 1 percent) who are wealthy in America. This group sees people who are seeking to do more than just be comfortable financially—those who are seeking to build legacy wealth—as doing it from a place of selfishness and narcissism. So they reject this as something they would personally pursue because they see it as unbefitting their ideals.

Finally, there are those who dream big about building wealth—but stop there. Or take action by playing the lottery or signing up for get-rich-quick schemes because they want the fast way to the riches. In this same group are all the unrealistic expectations for student athletes making it in the big leagues and people getting their big break in Hollywood. These are seen as the only legitimate paths to big money, because of ignorance or misinformation.

All of these views on wealth building miss a very critical point that is at the core of this book. This book is not about just money and how to make money. It's really about stewardship. Money is just one of the three areas of stewardship that we have all been charged with on this earth. The other two are our time and our talents.

In Psalm 24:1–2, we read that

> The earth is the Lord's, and everything in it,
> the world, and all who live in it;
> for he founded it on the seas
> and established it on the waters.

So if everything in the earth is the Lord's, it means that He owns it all, and we do not own anything. This goes way back to the Garden of Eden, when God gave Adam the job of taking care of His creation. We have always had the job of caretakers, not owners. God has entrusted us with the things that we have, but it is ultimately His purposes that need to be achieved through those things.

According to *Dictionary.com*, a steward is "a person who manages another's property or financial affairs; one who administers anything as the agent of another or others." Since we are the caretakers of His creation, we are the agents of God's affairs on earth; we are His stewards. This is the lens through which we should look at wealth building. When we build wealth ethically as God allows us, the goal is not our own gain but rather to walk in agreement with an ultimate purpose that He has for us to achieve through those resources. Combining the wealth that comes into our lives with our time and our talent ultimately brings about God's purpose in us. Falling short of what He intended us to do with what He gave us does the opposite; it hinders the purpose that He intended through us.

Ephesians 2:10 tells us what that purpose is: "we are God's handiwork, created in Christ Jesus to do good works, which God prepared in advance for us to do." The purpose for the wealth that God puts into our hands is to "do good works." Once we have taken care of the needs of our family and our children's children and we have a surplus, the proper response to the additional wealth He brings into our lives is to seek ways to be a blessing with that money.

My goal with this book is to help you move through five stages of financial being—from struggling to service—as quickly as possible so that you can move from being the one in need to being the one providing for those in need. This can happen only if you learn the correct principles for taking care of money and multiplying it so that you can multiply its impact in the world.

It's important to understand that this is bigger than you if you are going to operate in the fullness of God's expectation. I think the best way to illustrate this point is to open your mind about the three economic systems that impact your experience in the world.

The first economic system is God's system. In Matthew 6:26 Jesus tells us: "Look at the birds of the air; they do not sow or reap or store away in barns, and yet your heavenly Father feeds them. Are you not much more valuable than they?" As children of God, we are so valuable to Him that He will always provide for us. So we can look to Him and His economic system to provide for our needs, especially when we are struggling financially. In God's economic system, He is the ultimate provider.

Furthermore, in James 1:17 we read: "Every good and perfect gift is from above, coming down from the Father of the heavenly lights, who does not change like shifting shadows." From this scripture, we see two additional components of God's economic system. The first is that it is based on Him giving to us good and perfect gifts; if it comes from God, it is automatically perfect and good for us. The second is that His economic system is unwavering, because He is unwavering. So we can rely on it always being there for us. We don't have to worry about God's economic system going into recession, and everything He provides for us is good for us and exactly what we need.

Finally, in Genesis 12:2–4 we read the blessing that God gave to Abraham:

> I will make you into a great nation,
> and I will bless you;
> I will make your name great,
> and you will be a blessing.
> I will bless those who bless you,
> and whoever curses you I will curse;
> and all peoples on earth
> will be blessed through you.

Through Jesus, we were adopted into this blessing on Abraham that was passed down through generations. As Abraham was blessed, he would be a blessing to others, and ultimately all the peoples on earth would be blessed.

The final component I want to emphasize about God's economic system is that it is based on the passing on of blessings. He blesses us, we receive those blessings, and then we pass those blessings on to others. God's plan for bringing blessings into the world flows through our stewardship of the blessings that He gives to us.

God's economic system should be the system through which we see our financial lives, but we are often impacted by the other two: the world's economy and your personal economy. The world's economy is strongly based on borrowing and lending. Even nations owe other nations money. People borrow to get an education, to buy a car, to start a business, to buy a house, and even to pay off other money that they borrowed. Every time you borrow, you give your debtors power over what you do with the rest of the money that comes into your hands, because they have claim to a portion of it even before you have decided how to spend it. A debtor is tied to your future until you pay off the debt. When you operate in the economy of debt, it is very difficult to fully realize God's purpose for your stewardship.

Your personal economy is You Inc. It is the culmination of the financial decisions you have made throughout your life. If you have been aware of God's economic system for a while and have embraced it, this will be reflected in your personal economy and how your finances are faring. If you have been influenced more by the world's economy, this will also show.

Your personal economy dictates how well you're doing. If you have a job, then you think the economy is doing well. If you're not making any money, then you think the economy is doing poorly. But everybody has a personal economy that experiences ups and downs, just like the world economy has ups and downs. The key is to line up your personal economy with God's economy, now that you understand how God's economy works; then you can deal in the world's economy effectively because your personal economy will flourish as you take advantage of the right stewardship principles to be successful.

My hope is that this book will help you to make that connection by giving you the practical knowledge and tools you need to support the fulfillment of your God-given purpose as a steward of the treasure He has entrusted you with.

Chapter 2: Foundational Money Principles

THE SIMPLE BELIEVE ANYTHING, BUT THE PRUDENT GIVE
THOUGHT TO THEIR STEPS.

—Proverbs 18:21

For you to be successful in any area of your life, it is important to adopt a set of principles that are consistent with success in that area. Most of this book will focus on the mechanics of building wealth, but there are five key principles that are important for you to adopt if you are going to be successful. So I am dedicating this chapter to those principles before I teach you the strategies and tactics because I want you to connect with the wisdom behind the lessons and use these foundational principles as guides when you are faced with situations that I may not cover exactly how you experience them in your life. If you understand the principle and apply it, you will get the successful outcome.

The companion book to this one in the Ready, Set, Grow series focuses on principles that are critical to overall success in your life; the ones I will list here are specifically related to money. I will touch on some of them again throughout the book, but I thought it would be useful for you to have one place to go to for reference right at the beginning.

#1: Your Spending History Is Your TRUE Story

You can talk all you want about what is important to you, but the best way to really understand your priorities is to see where you spend your money. Repeat this several times to yourself: "My spending history is my TRUE story." Once this concept has crystallized in your mind, it will become easier to make more realistic plans with your money because you will not lie to yourself so much. You will not tell yourself that giving to charity is very important to you when in reality you give $50 to charity every year but spend $1,000 on shoes.

Another important component of this principle is that you have to start acting your WAGE. The same way there are certain places we spend less time in as we get older—and if we are found in those places, people tell us to act our age—when it comes to our finances, we have to act according to our income level. The only way to do this is to start tracking your expenses. Pay close attention in the chapter "Spending Control" to learn how to do this.

If you want to visualize the importance of acting your wage, think of running a race every month where you carry a bucket of water. When you get to the end of the race, you take a look at what you have left in the bucket. Imagine getting to the end of the race, and the bucket is empty. For some people, it's not even the end of the month; after two days they run out of water for the rest of the month, and then they have to borrow water from somebody else.

In Matthew 25:1, the Bible tells the parable of the ten virgins who went on a trip to meet the bridegroom. Five of them were wise enough to have a store of oil, so when the bridegroom took a long time to come, their lamps did not run out, because they had a chance to refuel. The five foolish virgins ran out of oil and asked the wise ones to help them, but the wise ones said that if they gave them oil, their own lamps would go out. This is similar to the situation where a person doesn't take care of saving for unforeseen circumstances and then needs to inconvenience a friend or family member to bail him or her out. Whenever you do that, you are being inconsiderate of the person whom you are asking for help, because his or her money has already been allocated to something else. When you request help in your crisis, you are forcing that person to forego something in his or her own plans.

Your budget is designed to give you a clear picture of the levels of spending you should be maintaining to ensure that you have enough to make it to the end of the month—and also save enough to deal with unforeseen circumstances. Later in the book when you learn how to properly create one, make sure to fill it out and start using it as soon as possible if you do not have a tracker like this already. Once you create a paper version, you can eventually graduate to managing your tracking online using a tool like Mint.com, but when you start out, writing things down by hand helps you to really address your spending issues directly.

#2: Move SLO (Spend It, Lend It, and Own Something)

When you earn a dollar, there are only three things you can do with it: spend it, lend it to somebody, or own something. All three choices have their place, but most people have mastered the first option and do not do as well with the other two.

Money principle #1 addressed spending, so let's take a look at lending money. The main way most people do this is by putting their money in the bank so that it can earn interest. When you put money in the bank, you are making a loan to the bank, and they take that money and reinvest it. The interest they pay you is their "rental fee" for using your money. This is not a very sound financial strategy for wealth building, because if you look at the interest rates for bank accounts, they are very low. Next time you get a bank statement, take a look at any of your accounts that earn interest, and add up how much you earn in a year. There are many people who don't make even $50 a year on the $100,000 they have in the bank. So even though this approach of lending is wiser than just spending the money you get, it is not the optimal strategy for all your money.

The third thing you can do with your money, ownership, is the most powerful way to bolster your finances and build wealth. When I say ownership, I am not talking about buying just anything, such as a bike or a car. You want to focus on buying assets that can appreciate in value—things that increase in value the longer you have them. Examples are stocks and real estate.

So every time you get a paycheck, think about moving SLO and really being deliberate about how your money is split between spending, lending, and owning. Your goals should be to put as much of your money as possible toward ownership after you have taken care of your spending priorities. This should be an ongoing exercise throughout your financial life to make sure that you always stay on track with your goals and continue to grow.

#3: Develop Your MIND

MIND stands for money, intelligence, need, and discipline. Each of these four areas needs to be consistently developed for you to be successful financially.

The first one, money, is just an object. What you have to learn to do is use it correctly to get what you need out of it and make it work properly. Everybody has money; what differs is the way we all manage our money. As you develop your ability to manage your money, your financial situation improves.

The second area, intelligence, refers to your money intelligence. Just as emotional intelligence determines how successful you are in your relationships, money intelligence determines how well you make decisions related to money—how "money smart" you are. As you increase your money intelligence, you see opportunities more clearly and avoid pitfalls more easily.

The third area, need, refers to developing a strong desire to be financially successful. Without this desire, you will not take the necessary actions (do the hard work) required for financial success. It is very similar to what determines whether you are successful with your health and fitness goals; if you lack a strong desire to make a change, you remain comfortable in your current state, even if it will lead to problems for you later in life.

The best way to develop your need is to become very clear about your goals. In the companion book to this one, *Set-4-Life*, I spend a lot of time talking about developing a vision and helping you break that vision down into tangible goals that can spur you into action. For example, if you have a goal to buy a house, you have to want to buy that house more than you want to go out to dinner every night with your friends, because both things pull on the same pool of money.

Finally, the D-word, here it comes: discipline. This one word is the cornerstone of success. You have to be able to commit to a course of action and see it through in order to be successful at anything, and that commitment requires discipline—the ability to do something even when you don't feel like doing it, because it is what you are supposed to do. It is no surprise that so many people say they are going to lose weight at the beginning of the year, or say they are going to start saving monthly—but never follow through. All they have done is said some words, but they have not put a timeline or a method of accountability to what they have said, so nothing gets done. They are waiting to do something someday, but someday never comes. When you read this book, part of your transformation should be to become one of the people who takes the steps necessary to back up what they say they are going to do.

#4: Do GOOD

This principle is very straightforward—get out of debt (GOOD), and then stay out of debt. Debt is the single biggest financial problem I have watched people struggle with in their financial lives. Using debt when you do not have the right financial discipline to take advantage of its benefits without falling prey to its detriments is very dangerous. Sadly, because of our high consumption culture, so many people fall into the arms of debt because they are trying to project a version of themselves that they believe is an expectation of their culture.

You may be reading this and saying to yourself, "I am not the kind of person who spends endlessly on handbags, shoes, or clothes. I don't spend money endlessly on gadgets, so I am not part of the consumption culture." Well, if you have a problem with debt—that means that you have debt outside of student loans[1]—then you are part of that consumption culture and need to reexamine your priorities.

In order to do GOOD, your goal should be to get out of debt as fast as possible, and I will show you some strategies to do so later in the book.

#5: Build a Farm, and Don't Kill Your Golden Goose

A farmer has two options if he wants to increase the number of his livestock and raise more animals. His first option is to buy more animals, and the second is to let his animals reproduce and organically increase their number. Buying more animals requires the farmer to continuously spend more, whereas if he focuses on maintaining the animals he already has and allows them to reproduce, they will increase in number with less additional spending by him. He is not limited to one approach at a time and can do both simultaneously if he chooses.

In the world of investing, buying more animals would be the same as taking a portion of your income and buying more assets, whereas allowing the animals to reproduce would be the same as accumulating the interest and dividends that grow from those investments or, if you are a landlord, collecting rent. As an investor, you want to use both strategies to grow your farm.

One of the biggest mistakes inexperienced investors make is to start killing off their livestock and eating their young before they have had a chance to reproduce—thus hindering their in-

---

[1] Business loans, car loans and mortgages can be "good debt" if you are doing the right business; or didn't buy too much car or too much house.

vestment power. This happens in the form of pulling the money out of their investments too soon in order to buy nonappreciating items—better described as "stuff." Another version of this behavior is using up all of your monthly income without putting any of it in assets, so you have no ability to reproduce from what you have earned.

If you have something that is producing income, you should do everything in your power to keep it producing income and even increase the income. If you have a job, work hard at it and show up on time. If you have a property, take care of it because that upkeep will help the golden goose lay more eggs; don't sell it and cut off the income. That is like eating your young.

I learned that phrase—"eating your young"—while I was in college. One summer, I worked at an audiovisual job, and a gentleman came into one of my rooms to teach about investing in stock options. I helped him set up for his presentation and was fascinated by all of the investment strategies he explained during his class. At the end of it, I walked up to him and asked, "Is this legal?"

He said, "Yeah, why?"

I said, "If this is legal, and people can invest money like this and make money, why are people in debt? Why doesn't everybody do this?"

He said, "Well, even if everybody knew this, they wouldn't all apply it."

From that day forth, I started learning from him how to invest. He worked at the Chicago Board Options Exchange, and I used to call him up for investment advice to learn more and make the right trading decisions. My initial investment was about $2,000, and by the end of the summer, I had done very well and had grown it to over $10,000. I still remember calling for my balance; we didn't have any way to check online then. The total balance was

$10,228.42. I couldn't believe what I heard, so I pressed one to hear the recording again. It said $10,241.21.

I was so excited that I called in and told them to sell all the investments and send me the money. And as any young man would do with that money, I decided to have a good time. I flew to Atlanta to a big party for fraternities and sororities. While there, I spent the money on things such as a big hotel room and eating out every night and ordering everything à la carte. I was a high roller.

Two weeks later, I called my gentleman friend in the usual way for advice on what to trade and buy, and he asked me, "What are you investing in?"

I said, "Oh, I took the money out and spent about three of the ten thousand."

Without hesitation, he said, "You're eating your young"—and hung up.

I never forgot that lesson. I had something that was producing income, and I sold it and spent it on something that wasn't. From that day forward, it has been very hard for me to sell something that is producing income. I actually want to produce more of it. That is probably part of the reason why I am writing this book and teaching you this: I want you to learn how to produce and make more.

To avoid the mistake of eating your young, make sure to put money into your assets every month. Even if your assets are real estate, you can put money into them by paying the mortgage down faster or fixing up the property. What you don't want to do is to kill your golden goose.

Think of every asset you buy as a golden goose. The objective is to benefit from the golden eggs that the asset produces, but the goose can produce those eggs only when it is alive. If you kill your goose by spending the principal of your investment, selling the real estate, or drawing too much money out of your business, you will stop benefitting from its golden eggs because it will no longer be around to produce them for you.

Instead, think of ways to help your goose produce even more eggs. With an investment portfolio, this might be rebalancing the investments to yield a better return. For real estate, it might be consolidating a set of properties into a single property that has a much better cash flow. For a business, it might be using your creativity to come up with more products or market to a group of people you have not served before. In each instance, you hold on to the golden goose, the principal, but you find ways to make it reproduce at a higher level for you.

This is probably the most important money principle for building wealth.

Take Action:

Examine Your Principles

Take a moment and reflect on each of the principles I listed in this chapter. Write down for yourself the answer to these two questions:

1. Which of the principles will be the hardest for me to adopt?

2. How can I do a little something today to start operating with that principle instead of the way I have in the past?

Chapter 3

The Wealth Map

Why People Stay Broke

THE TONGUE HAS THE POWER OF LIFE AND DEATH,
AND THOSE WHO LOVE IT WILL EAT ITS FRUIT.

—Proverbs 18:21

SOW A THOUGHT, REAP A WORD; SOW A WORD,
REAP A DEED; SOW A DEED, REAP A HABIT; SOW A HABIT,
REAP A CHARACTER; SOW A CHARACTER, REAP A DESTINY.

—Unknown

D*ictionary.com* describes the adjective version of the word "broke" as "without money—penniless." It also provides an idiom, "go broke," which means "to become destitute of money or possessions." If those definitions are not sufficient for your understanding, you can always go over to

UrbanDictionary.com and read the definition there with its contemporary sample sentence:

Definition: the state of having no or very little money...being penniless, out of cash.

> *Hey dude, you coming to the club for a drink Saturday?*
> *Nah man, I'm broke.*

From the serious to the tongue in cheek, the outcome is the same when we talk about being broke: the money you have is not sufficient for what you believe you need to live or even survive. The reason I am taking the time to write a section on being broke and why so many people stay that way is that over the years, of the people that I have worked with on their personal finances, I have observed a subset whose situation never seems to improve. I work with them for a while, help them to get all the right information and take the right actions, but after a few years, or even a few months, they are back to the crisis financial situation they started out with. Sometimes their situation is worse than when we started working together.

Now, in some cases, there is a meaningful reason that this happens; an unforeseen event such as a serious medical situation or the loss of a job can set people's financial plans back and potentially put them in a worse position than they were in when they started proactively managing their money. But I am not talking about this type of situation. This section of the book refers to those cases where people continuously gravitate toward a state of "broke-ness" despite getting all the right financial education and knowing the right things to do.

I have spent a lot of time thinking about this situation and why it exists and have come to the following conclusion: being broke is a mind-set. When we observe people who are caught in this cycle of being broke, what is visible to us are their behaviors, but what we cannot see are their beliefs, because those are internal and are sometimes not clear even to them.

If you try to change your behavior without changing your beliefs, your results will be temporary. You may do well for a season, but eventually, your subconscious mind will bring you back to where your beliefs lie. As the first quote at the beginning of the chapter shows, the ultimate driver of what we do consistently is how we think—and how we think is driven by our beliefs.

So the best way to explain why people stay broke is to talk about the broke beliefs that underlie the broke behavior. People stay broke because of beliefs they hold in one or more of the following areas:

- Beliefs about themselves
- Beliefs about money
- Beliefs about their relationships
- Beliefs about work
- Beliefs about failure
- Beliefs about responsibility

In the first area of belief, people stay broke because their self-esteem is low, and therefore they do not believe that they are worthy of wealth. Or they resign themselves to mediocrity because they do not believe they have the capability to acquire wealth. Both of these beliefs cause them to operate their financial lives with no goals, or very small goals. After all, how can you make a goal to build wealth if you don't believe you are worthy or capable of doing so? The result of operating their financial lives with no goals is that they are often spectators of their own lives, watching things happen to them and waiting for somebody else to intervene to help resolve their situation. This is a position of powerlessness that further perpetuates their belief that they are unworthy and incapable.

The second area of belief is the way that people who are constantly broke think about money. The first type of broke belief about money is what I call the "when I get it, I spend it" mentality. This is the belief that when you get money, your only option is to spend it. I address this mentality in detail later in the book, but what I would mention here is that it is what leads to the bondage of debt that hinders people's ability to build wealth. Without getting their spending under control, people with the "when I get it, I spend it" mentality often live above their means and therefore have to borrow just to maintain their lifestyle.

Another belief about money that causes people to stay broke is the mental anchors they have about what they are able to earn. If you think that $30,000 a year is a lot, chances are you will never earn more than that until you expand your belief about what is possible for you. You can say the same thing about any income level; some people's anchor is six figures, and so they can grow their income all the way to the high $90,000s but can't seem to get past the $100,000 mark. This belief about what is possible in terms of income is closely tied to the self-esteem issue I described earlier, and the only way to break out of it is to grow your beliefs about what you are worth.

When it comes to the third area, beliefs about relationships, there are two traps that I have seen people fall into. The first is the belief that "yes" means "I love you." This belief is the reason that people allow friends, family, and relatives to determine their financial future, because they are always lending money to or co-signing loans for the people close to them. The other form of this belief is when parents allow their grown children to live in their home indefinitely and don't hold them accountable for working on a plan to move out. In both instances, people believe that they are showing love by being so generous, but what they are really doing in most cases is hindering the development of the other person. In the case of adult children, you are hindering their ability to become an independent adult because instead of empowering them to grow, you are enabling their immaturity.

You can see an extension of this problem even with children who are still minors. Doing things such as buying a two-year-old designer clothes has nothing to do with what is best for the child. You don't spend money on your children; you invest in them. Instead of buying them a whole bunch of toys (some toys are okay, but we are all guilty of overdoing it), we invest in them by taking them to karate class, getting them into good schools, and spending money for them on things that have longevity.

The other broke belief about relationships happens when people are too worried about what other people think about them. They have a belief that somehow their worth is tied to how much other people like and respect them. This leads to the "keeping up with the Joneses" mentality, where they incur expenditures that are above their means in order to appear successful according to somebody else's definition.

The fourth broke belief is related to the way a person views work. I've always found it interesting that people who are wealthy do not just sit back and stop being productive after they reach a certain level of wealth. By contrast, people who are broke are the ones who are often looking for ways to get out of work or for a shortcut to making money that will require less work. This is where people get caught up in get-rich-quick scams; because of their greed and poor work ethic, they would rather try to find a shortcut to wealth than do the hard work that it takes to build wealth.

The broke belief about work extends to daydreaming about the lottery and spending money on those tickets instead of using that same money to improve your financial situation. The odds of winning in the lottery are so low that you might as well take the money you spend on tickets and burn it each time you get the urge to play. In fact, the bigger the jackpot, the more this is true, because then the more people decide to play.

The fifth broke belief is the belief that failure should be avoided. This is a mind-set that may look healthy on the outside, because people are always cautious about what they do with their money, but it also means that they have no appetite for risk. So they avoid any type of investing because they could potentially lose the money, and therefore cut themselves off from building wealth. They also don't take any chances to increase their income by trying for a bigger, better job, or branching out and going into real estate or starting a side business. Understand that failure is unavoidable and the healthiest attitude toward it is to think of it as the disclaimer you find on a mutual fund—"Past performance is not indicative of future results"—meaning that if something was bad in the past, that doesn't mean it's going to be bad in the future.

The last area of broke beliefs has to do with responsibility. People who are broke tend to believe that things happen to them; they see the reason for their situation as something that is being done or was done to them. They are very good at making excuses for why they are in their current situation and don't take the time to see how they are a big part of the problem. Without this ability to introspect, they are never able to truly make the adjustments that are needed to move from being broke to building wealth.

So now that you know each of these belief areas and how they could be keeping you or people you know broke, don't spend any time beating yourself or them up about what you have learned. The reason I shared all this information is that before I start teaching about any principles or mechanics for building wealth, I want you to understand clearly how much of the work is going to have to be in your mind. Make a commitment today to be honest with yourself about any of the beliefs that may be keeping you broke and to use the techniques in this book's companion book, *Set-4-Life*, to help you develop the right mind-set and habits to be successful.

A Map to Set Your Course

SUPPOSE ONE OF YOU WANTS TO BUILD A TOWER.
WON'T YOU FIRST SIT DOWN AND ESTIMATE THE COST
TO SEE IF YOU HAVE ENOUGH MONEY TO COMPLETE IT?

—Luke 14:28

Have you ever been to a mall that you have never shopped in before? On the outside, you can usually see the anchor stores, the biggest stores on either end, but once you get inside and try to find the store you are looking for, it can sometimes seem like quite a maze.

Mall designers know that if a potential customer gets lost in the mall, it decreases the chances of that person making a purchase, so they are highly motivated to ensure that it is easy for people to find what they are looking for and know where to go. That is why every mall has several strategically placed directories with a map of the mall and a list of all the stores with a color and number code to help you find the one that you need.

I feel the same way about this book. Resetting for a new beginning will lose its power very quickly if you do not have a solid guide on what to do once you have a clean slate. I have therefore come up with my own directory, called the Wealth Map, that will guide you through the maze of personal finance and ensure that you can locate yourself at any given moment. Throughout the book I will refer to this guide to keep you focused on the most important elements to master.

And just like the directories in the mall have a "You Are Here" sticker to show you your starting point, once I share this map with you here briefly, I will show you how to determine where you are.

The Wealth Map has three sections that help you navigate your financial journey:

- The five levels of financial being
- The five keys to achievement
- The four stages of financial growth

All the sections work together and need to be developed progressively to get your desired outcomes. The reason I structured the map this way is because I truly believe financial well-being requires a holistic approach in both content and process.

The five levels of financial being are like the "You Are Here" sticker. They help you to locate your current financial position, because not everybody is starting from the same place. As you learn more about these levels, you will naturally place yourself in one of them and therefore know what actions are most relevant to you.

The five keys to achievement are like the skeleton of your financial body; without them, the strategies you put in place will flop over like a body made up of skin and muscle but no bones. Mastering these keys will make you successful not only financially but in all areas of your life. The content for this section of the map is the focus of the other book in the series, *Set-4-Life: The Mindset of a Champion*, where you will learn how to take advantage of the keys to accelerate your financial future.

The four stages of financial growth are the milestones that help you move through the five levels. Each stage builds on the previous stage, and the stronger you get in each area, the more your wealth will develop.

THE WEALTH MAP

THE 5 LEVELS OF FINANCIAL BEING

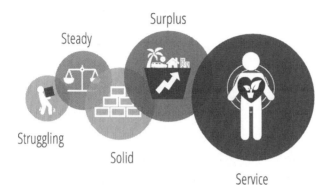

Surplus

Steady

Struggling

Solid

Service

THE 5 KEYS TO ACHIEVEMENT

MIND	BODY	GOALS	HABITS	OUTCOMES
VISION	VEHICLE	PLAN	SYSTEM	METRICS
Principles Character	Words Actions	Pathway	Consistency	Accountability

Knowledge

Action

THE 4 STAGES OF FINANCIAL GROWTH

1 Spending Control

2 Debt Elimination

3 SaVesting

4 Building a Wealth Machine

Figure 1: The Wealth Map

Five Levels of Financial Being

In order to change your circumstances, you have to be very clear about where you are and where you want to go. The first step in this transformation process is to assess your current circumstances so you can accurately decide your next steps. In this book, the Five Levels of Financial Being are the guideline that helps you make that assessment correctly.

Level 1: Struggling

In its simplest terms, "struggling" is the inability to pay your bills. Every month you have more month than money, and you get further behind as time passes. It's as if you have to bring your family water from the river, but there is a hole in your bucket, and by the time you get home, the water is gone. Here's an example of this situation: one of our clients doesn't have anything left over when she finishes paying for rent, utilities, food, and groceries. When her car breaks down, she puts the expense on a credit card, and when that is maxed out, she borrows from friends and family. She is constantly in a crisis mode.

The key goal in the struggling stage is to find a way to stop the financial bleeding. You need to plug the hole in the bucket so that it can actually carry the water home to your family.

Level 2: Steady

At this level, you make just enough money to pay your bills, but there is nothing left over for saving and investing. This means that if anything catastrophic happens to your income or expenses, you easily fall back into the struggling level because you have nothing to bridge the gap. An even more common scenario is that you have not saved enough for college or retirement, and when those major life events come up, it's a crisis. This is a very precarious position to be in, but sadly it's where most Americans are regardless of how well they think they are doing. A survey released by Bankrate.com in 2013 concluded that 76 percent of US households are living paycheck to paycheck.[2] Even more distressing in that survey was that 27 percent had no savings at all. A recent follow-up to that survey showed that not much had changed even with the improving economy.[3] People's financial priorities are still things such as "staying current on living expenses" or "getting caught up on bills."

The key to moving forward from this stage is to increase your cash flow so that you can have a surplus to start saving and investing.

Level 3: Solid

"Solid" means that you are able to breathe financially. You have enough to pay your bills, take a one-week vacation without taking on debt, put money into your 401(k), and give charitable contributions to your church and any other organizations you support. Basically, you have a good foundation for your longer-term financial goals and can meet most of the short-term ones without too much effort.

Here is the next reality check. There are many people who believe they are solid when under the covers they are just a strong steady. This happens when you have not factored your long-term financial goals, such as college costs and retirement, into your

[2] http://money.cnn.com/2013/06/24/pf/emergency-savings/

[3] http://www.bankrate.com/finance/consumer-index/saving-money-remains-low-priority-in-us.aspx

overall plan. It looks as if you are meeting your monthly budget quite well, but this is an illusion, because you are not saving at a high-enough rate to avoid a panic later on.

Level 4: Surplus

Surplus is quite simply extra money that isn't already needed to meet one of your foundational financial priorities. And you get to ponder and decide what happens to it without putting yourself in harm's way. Another way to think about surplus is that your decisions about whether to do something are not limited by your income. People at this level are typically business owners and invest their money to make it work for them.

Level 5: Service

Service is the highest level, and it means that you do not find yourself thinking about money. You just do whatever is God's purpose for your life and are not worried about day-to-day finances. At this level, your mind is freed up to dream really big dreams, and you have the ability to put those dreams into motion because you have the resources to back them without looking for a loan or handout.

Now that you know the five levels, it's time to pinpoint yourself on the Wealth Map. You need to assess your current situation so that you can align the starting point of your journey with the path that will take you to your goals. The best way to do this assessment is to calculate two numbers:

- Your monthly cash flow
- Your net worth

Calculating your monthly cash flow will force you to look at how money flows in and out of your life. This will give you a good sense of how much or how little control you have of your budget. Calculating your net worth will give you insight into how much debt you have and how far you are from your longer-term financial goals.

Go to http://www.yourwealthcycle.com/worksheets and print off the Monthly Cash Flow and Net Worth worksheets to calculate both numbers.

Once you have done these calculations, you should fill out the Five Levels Assessment at http://www.yourwealthcycle.com/mylevel as honestly as possible (there is an abbreviated version in the Take Action section coming up). Cheating only hurts you and hinders you from growing, so be as brutally truthful as possible. The total score from this assessment will tell you your current level.

Take Action: Identify Your Level

Read the following characteristics and pick the level that best describes your current financial situation:

Characteristics	Your Level
▸ You are always short of money at the end of the month ▸ You are waiting for something to 'happen' to be able to pay your bills (e.g. waiting for a tax return) ▸ You are constantly borrowing money from people ▸ You are worried about money/finances all the time	Struggling
▸ You have JUST enough to pay your bills ▸ You feel like you are 'treading water' financially ▸ If anything happens (snap, crackles or pops), you will be back to drowning financially and have to 'come up for air' ▸ You are always just at the brink of a financial crisis ▸ If you have one negative financial event, you will be back to struggling	Steady
▸ You typically have been working somewhere for a while ▸ You have reserves / emergency fund ▸ You are tithing and giving generously ▸ You are able to go on a one week vacation with your family without using debt ▸ You are consistently paying into your retirement fund and may even have some other investments in the stock market	Solid

Characteristics	Your Level
▶ You have extra money ▶ You have been working somewhere for a while ▶ You have the same characteristics as solid, but in addition, most of your decisions are driven by whether or not you want to do something (not how much money it will take) ▶ You most likely own a business and/or some investment real estate in addition to your stock market investments	Surplus
▶ You are not concerned about money for day-to-day things ▶ You are thinking about being a philantropist ▶ You are less worried about how to increase your income, and more concerned about paying less taxes ▶ You are thinking about how to 'pass things on', build a legacy	Service

If you would like a more rigorous approach, you can fill out the test at http://www.yourwealthcycle.com/mylevel and find out what I think your level is based on your answers.

Once you know your level, write it down here:

You may be surprised by the outcome. You might think you should be at a higher level, or be pleasantly surprised that you are not as low as you thought. Regardless of your level, do not get too emotionally worked up about it; this is just data that you can use as a starting point. I have a plan to help you regardless of your level using the four stages of financial growth.

The Four Stages of Financial Growth

Once you are clear on your level of financial being, the next question on your mind would naturally be "How do I get better?" If you are struggling, you want to know how to get to steady; if you are steady, you want to know how to get to solid; and so on. The purpose of the four stages of financial growth is to help you navigate the five levels with specific actions and goals that will build on each other to make sure you are successful. Each stage is designed to move you from one level to the next.

The four stages are as follows:

- Spending Control
- Debt Elimination
- SaVesting
- Building a Wealth Machine

The first three stages build on each other, and the last one helps you grow exponentially. The order in which you complete the stages is therefore much more important for the first three than for the last one. In later chapters of this book, I will go into more details about the action steps you need to take in each of the stages, but for now here is a short summary about what each one is about.

Stage 1: Spending Control

Managing a budget and spending wisely are the cornerstone skills to any financial success. If you do not master this stage, you will always have a rocky foundation that can come tumbling down at any moment. This stage is the critical focus for anybody who is in a crisis struggling situation. Cutting down on your spending and living on a strict budget are critical to stop struggling. You need the next stage to move from struggling to solid.

Stage 2: Debt Elimination

Based on the statistics I shared earlier, if you are struggling, chances are part of your problem is your monthly debt payments. So if you lower and eventually eliminate the payments on your credit cards, student loans, and car, you significantly improve your financial situation. You can go from not having enough money to fulfill your monthly obligations to at least balancing your budget each month.

Stage 3: SaVesting

If you are currently steady and want to move to solid, your focus should be to simultaneously increase your saving and investing. The two work together because as you increase your cash flow through better spending habits and debt elimination, you have more money to put toward your savings and investments. There are two sides to increasing your cash flow: increasing your income and decreasing your expenses. If you have done a good job in stage 2 of eliminating debt, the extra money you free up because you no longer have to pay on your debt can give you a significant boost in your cash flow.

In addition, if you haven't already done so in the struggling level, this is when to consider picking up extra work part-time or as a freelancer. The more income you can bring into your household, while keeping your expenses low, the faster you will move from steady to solid.

Stage 4: Building a Wealth Machine

Once you are comfortably in the solid level—all your bills are covered, and you are saving sufficiently for all your long-term and short-term priorities, while doing some basic investing—it's time to accelerate your wealth-building process. This is where the skills of building a wealth machine come into play. You use this wealth machine to move you from solid to surplus.

The Advanced Stages: Real Estate, Business, and Giving Back

Once you are in a place of surplus, your financial potential is wide open. You can choose to focus on building businesses, managing a real estate portfolio, or both. As you use these advanced investment tools, your capacity for philanthropy and good deeds grows, and it is important that you invest in those who need assistance and are not yet at your stage. The ultimate expression of your financial growth is giving back.

Now that you have your map, you know where you are on the map, and you have a basic understanding of what you need to focus on to move forward, it's time to discuss the Wealth Cycle and how it can help you transform your financial life in a systematic and organized way.

Chapter 4:

What Is the Wealth Cycle?

AND GOD IS ABLE TO BLESS YOU ABUNDANTLY, SO THAT
IN ALL THINGS AT ALL TIMES, HAVING ALL THAT YOU NEED,
YOU WILL ABOUND IN EVERY GOOD WORK.

—2 Corinthians 9:8

TRUE WEALTH IS NOT MEASURED IN MONEY OR STATUS OR
POWER. IT IS MEASURED IN THE LEGACY WE LEAVE BEHIND
FOR THOSE WE LOVE AND THOSE WE INSPIRE.

—Cesar Chavez

Building wealth is much less about income than it is about
cash flow. The fundamental difference between somebody
at the struggling level and somebody at the service level is
that the latter has more discretionary financial resources to work
with. Two people can have high six-figure incomes, but one of
them can still be struggling because the amount of his or her bills
is just as high as the amount of money coming in whereas the
other person is steadily building wealth.

Building wealth is also a cyclical process. People do not become wealthy from a single event such as winning the lottery, because wealth building requires some critical skills and processes that can only be mastered over time. It is a well-known fact that when people win what they consider a fortune in the lottery, there is a good chance that a few years down the line, they will have spent all of that money and be back to the same place they started financially. The reason is that although they had money at their disposal, they did not possess the skills or know the processes to turn that money into wealth. According to the Bible, in Proverbs 13:22, real wealth is multigenerational—"A good person leaves an inheritance for their children's children"—so to say that you have truly built wealth, you have to have a plan in place that ensures this wealth will be around for your grandchildren to enjoy.

Now that we have established that building wealth is not an event, the next thing to understand is what exactly this cyclical process looks like. In the past when I have taught the principles of wealth building, I have provided several helpful tools, such as my Debt Eliminator and my 100 Ways to Save, but what I have realized over time is that these things are most powerful when they are understood in the context of the overall process and how it works. This is especially true because the process is used by not only beginners in wealth building but also those who are advanced and have already built up a sizeable net worth. My reflections on how all this fits together are captured and best taught by introducing and describing to you the Wealth Cycle.

The Wealth Cycle is a four-point process supported by simple but powerful tools that will help you to navigate your wealth-building journey in an organized, thoughtful, and effective way. Though the concepts composing the Wealth Cycle are easy to understand, their real power comes from implementing them, and that is where you will find the largest areas of growth and challenges for yourself as you work through each component.

The four points in the process are as follows:

- Monitor your cash flow
- Analyze your cash flow
- Increase your cash flow
- Distribute your cash flow

What ties the four pieces together is that they all refer to the critical element of all wealth building that I mentioned before: cash flow. In fact, if you are a visual person, the Wealth Cycle looks like this:

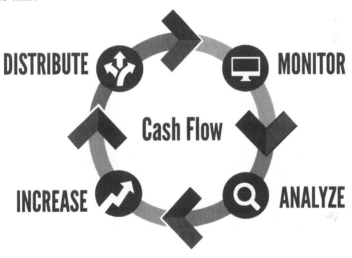

Figure 2: The Wealth Cycle

So let's go ahead and do a high-level breakdown of the Wealth Cycle before we go into specifics. Because I think it is critical that you understand each of these areas before we start talking about strategies, I will start with a very basic understanding of cash flow, since it is the lifeblood of the whole thing.

What Is Cash Flow?

No matter how you look at it, whether it is written on a napkin at a dinner table or displayed in some fancy charts and graphs in an expensive personal-finance application, when you strip it down to its essentials, cash flow is just a mathematical equation. Don't worry; you don't have to be a master of calculus to understand that equation, because even a seven-year-old knows how to do this math:

Cash Flow = Income − Spending

I know I am making it sound overly simplistic, but I am doing so on purpose to make a point. People often act as if the reason they are struggling financially were a mystery that can be solved only by Sherlock Holmes, when the truth always comes back to whether that equation is consistently positive, and if it isn't, why not.

In fact, we can take a look at how the parts of the equation apply to each of the five levels of financial being so that you can start to see how all this comes together.

Here is how each level looks:

Table 1: Cash flow and the Five Levels

Struggling	Spending > Income	Cash flow is negative every month because borrowing/debt is needed to pay all obligations.
Steady	Spending = Income	Cash flow is zero, so no savings or investments.
Solid	Spending < Income	Cash flow is positive, and saving/basic investing is possible.
Surplus	Spending <<< Income	Cash flow is significantly positive, and there is no debt.
Service	Spending <<< Passive income	Cash flow from investments, real estate, and businesses creates significant passive and residual income.

In plain English, people who are struggling have an inability to pay their basic bills. People who are steady can pay their basic bills but don't have enough to consistently save. People who are solid are doing well because they have an emergency fund, they're saving at least 10 percent of their income, they're giving 10 percent of their income to their church or to charity, and they have money remaining to enjoy by, for example, taking a one-week vacation. People in surplus have all the things that people in solid have and then some. And people in service are not concerned about money; they do what God has placed them on this earth to do because they have sources of income that don't require them to spend their time working.

When you put it in these simple terms, it is very easy to figure out which level you are on by tallying up all of your monthly income sources and then comparing them to how much you spend every month. The exercise is not very difficult in terms of brain power, but it is very emotional for people who are still in the struggling or steady stages because it requires them to face difficult truths about their habits and potentially misplaced priorities. People who are solid to service have gotten there because they understand the power of the equation and have created ways to keep a pulse on their cash flow consistently, which brings us to the first of the four points in the Wealth Cycle: monitor your cash flow.

Monitor Your Cash Flow

Before you can make any strides in your wealth-building journey, you have to become very good at understanding where your money goes. Believe it or not, to a large number of people, the answer to "Where does your money go?" is not very clear, and they therefore feel powerless to take control of their financial situation.

You have to learn how to move SLO. When you earn a dollar, there are only three things you can do with it. All three choices have their place, but most people have mastered the first option and do not do as well with the others. Besides holding on to it and maybe hiding it under your mattress, the three things are as follows:

1. **Spend it.** This is the one everybody has mastered—buying things that are consumable or don't grow in value.
2. **Lend it.** This means that you put it in the bank and let it earn interest.
3. **Own something.** This is the key to wealth building. The more of your dollars that can be redirected to ownership, the more wealth you will build over time.

Your money is going to one of those three areas, and you have to start monitoring how much you are putting into each area.

To get at the heart of what it means to monitor, we first have to discuss the concept of living beneath your means. Your means is the mechanism by which you maintain a living; it is the substance that supports your lifestyle. In America, there is an epidemic of people living above their means. The best way to see how this may play out is to give you a fictitious example that may sound very similar either to your own situation or to that of someone you know.

Let's compare two neighbors who earn exactly the same income but make drastically different choices about where that income goes. Goodwin H. Bucks and Donald N. Spender both work as salesmen earning salary and commission that total $75,000 per year. Don is determined to live better than his neighbor, and as a result he has added two new rooms to his home. He owns a luxury vehicle and an SUV. He has put a pool in his backyard, and he's planning a trip to Europe in the summer. His suits are custom made, and his wife is looking for her third fur coat. Even his young children have the best designer clothes money can buy. Unfortunately, his yearly income of $75,000 does not support such an extravagant lifestyle, and Don has hit the limit on all of his credit cards. He is taking out a second mortgage on his home, he has borrowed thousands from his wife's family, and his bank loans exceed $10,000.

By contrast, his neighbor Goodwin is content with his home in its original state and uses his commission checks to add to his investment portfolio on top of contributing the maximum to his 401(k) plan. He saves a total of 25 percent of his gross income, has paid off his two vehicles, and pays cash for all of his purchases. Goodwin and his family are flying to a summer resort using tickets he purchased with the frequent flyer miles he accumulated through his sales travels. Goodwin's wife has a home-based business, and the additional funds she generates go toward their children's college fund. Since the Buckses have decided to live on one paycheck, they have saved six months of Goodwin's salary for an emergency.

As you can see, the net worth of each family is drastically different. Goodwin's net worth continues to climb steadily as his investments grow, his savings increase, and his future becomes more and more secure. On the other hand, Donald continues to sink deeper into debt. He must continue to borrow money to maintain a lifestyle that is consistently above his means. His spending far exceeds the actual amount he takes home, and he must find additional means of income. However, he has not considered getting a second job and has instead opted to find additional ways to borrow to keep up with his voracious spending.

Many people believe that if they had more money, they would not be in debt, but as you can see from the two neighbors, the amount of income does not determine your net worth. It is the manner in which you use that money and how much of it you keep. The income standard is relative.

I shared that detailed story with you because I want you to truly understand how important it is to live beneath your means and not above or even at your means. One of the biggest misconceptions held by most people is that success equals living at their means. They don't understand that if you are living at your means, spending every penny, you are actually living above your means because you are not saving a minimum of 10 percent of your income and therefore have no provision for future plans or unexpected expenses that WILL come up.

The way you ensure that you know what your means are, so that you can make sure you live below them, is by keeping track of what you spend. That is the essence of the Monitor component of the Wealth Cycle. You must have a systematic way to consistently check in on the different places that your money is going and make any necessary adjustments. Money that is unmonitored will take on a life of its own, and before you know it, you will not be tracking toward your larger goals as you expected.

The tool that you use to monitor is your budget—a written plan of how you intend to spend your money. But a budget does not work for the monitoring role if you do not compare it to your actual spending. So along with your budget, you need a reliable way to account for all the money that you spend, and a consistent weekly check-in to compare the two. If you are married, it is important that the budget be created by both of you and that the weekly check-ins is done together.

We will take a deeper look at how to create an effective budget later, but for now the thing to note is that it is important to look at all the places that your money is going and separate them into three categories: installment debt, life expenses (budget), and prosperity dollars. These three areas form the foundation of the next component of the Wealth Cycle: analyze your cash flow.

Analyze Your Cash Flow

If you are still reading, I know that you would like to see some change in your life financially. Change is possible only if you know what actions to take, and in order to know what actions to take, you need to understand where your problems reside. When it comes to wealth building, you have to analyze your cash flow to know what your next steps should be, because they are different depending on which level of financial being you are operating at.

Over the years, I have developed a tool called Money in Motion that I think is a simple but very powerful way to give you a clear analysis of your cash flow and show where your focus should be in your wealth-building journey. The Money in Motion tool includes the three categories in the table below:

Installment debt	Budget	Prosperity dollars

Figure 3: Money in Motion

To fill it out, you look across all your expenditures and fill in the monthly amounts that you spend in each of these areas:

- **Installment debt.** This includes credit cards, investment property mortgages, car loans, student loans, and any other debt in your life.

- **Life expenses (budget).** This includes all the money you spend on yourself and your household, such as groceries, food, entertainment, cable, and so on.
- **Prosperity dollars.** This is all the money you spend on giving, future savings, and investments such as brokerage accounts, 401(k)s, 403(b)s, and IRAs, as well as how much equity you are building in your home.

When it is filled out, it looks something like this:

Installment debt	Budget	Prosperity dollars
Major credit card #1	Mortgage/ rent payment	Giving
Major credit card #2	Cable	401(k)
Department store card #1	Utilities	403(b) TSA
Department store card #2	Telephone	Brokerage account
Car loan	Food / groceries / eating out	Education
Student loan	Entertainment	Home equity
TOTAL $$	TOTAL $$	TOTAL $$

Putting each of these areas side by side will give you a total for each column, and you will quickly be able to see where most of your money is going and how that impacts your ability to build wealth. If you have a lot of money going to installment debt and barely any to prosperity dollars, you are in the same situation as Donald N. Spender and his family: you are most likely struggling financially. If you have more money going to your prosperity dollars and low to zero funds going to installment debt, you are more like Goodwin H. Bucks and his family: you are in a solid financial place.

In fact, this tool is a very helpful way to understand what it means to be in each of the five levels of financial being, as illustrated in this table:

Level	Installment debt	Budget	Prosperity dollars
Struggling	High	High	Zero
Steady	High	High	Low
Solid	Low	Low	Medium
Surplus	Zero	Low	High
Service	Zero	Low	High[4]

**Figure 4: Relative Portion of Income
Directed to Money in Motion Category**

When you break down your financial situation in the Money in Motion table, you can begin to pinpoint the problem areas that you need to work on to move to the next level. For each of the levels, the remedy is to increase your cash flow, but the ways you can do so differ based on your level. Increasing your cash flow is what the next level of the Wealth Cycle helps you do.

Increase Your Cash Flow

There are only two ways you can increase your cash flow: either lower your expenses or increase the amount of money coming into your life. When people fall into financial trouble, they often focus too much on the need to increase the money coming

---

[4] Though surplus and service will look the same in Money in Motion, the real distinction between the two is not monetary but related to time freedom/flexibility.

in, without taking a close-enough look at how much is going out and how they can change that portion of the equation. In fact, they often make the outflow section of the equation bigger by taking on more debt instead of lowering it.

Perhaps a picture will help with this concept. In the Increase portion of the Wealth Cycle, there are two types of action to take:

Figure 5: Ways to Increase Cashflow

You need to *decrease* your expenses and debt and *increase* your income. This is simple to say, but it is much more challenging to put into practice. Over the years, while teaching personal finance, I have developed some tools to help people focus on the left side of the equation early on and then eventually move to the right side where they increase their income.

To decrease expenses, I have developed a comprehensive list of tips and examples that can help you save like a pro. In the SaVesting chapter, you will learn how to save depending on which of the five levels you are currently in. Before the SaVesting section, I am going to teach you about one of the most powerful tools I have used to help people transform their financial situation: the Debt Eliminator. This is a systematic way you can eliminate debt once and for all so that you can move on to truly building your wealth without carrying a weight that slows you down. These two sections on debt elimination and SaVesting are most transformational for people in the struggling and steady stages, but I also have tips for people who are in the later stages, because as I said before, the Wealth Cycle is something that you continuously go through.

For people in the solid to service levels, the Increase section of their Wealth Cycle still contains elements of saving and debt elimination, but a much greater focus goes into income growth so that they can exponentially increase their wealth. This is the primary focus of the chapter "Building a Wealth Machine" and is the basis for the main goal of the fourth section of the Wealth Cycle: distribute your cash flow.

Distribute Your Cash Flow

Once you have gone through the steps of monitoring, analyzing, and increasing your cash flow, the next step is to distribute your surplus money into the right vehicles. In the example I used to explain living beneath your means, a critical component of why the two families were in such drastically different places financially was their decisions about where to distribute their cash flow. This idea takes us full circle to the fundamental concept I started this chapter with: spend it, lend it, or own something.

In the Distribute portion of the Wealth Cycle, you are consistently looking for ways to direct your cash flow toward ownership. This is initially through simple investments in the stock market and homeownership for the struggling and steady stages, then grows into more sophisticated investing and business ownership for the solid, surplus, and service stages. The idea is to continuously build up multiple sources of income so that you build a powerful wealth machine that eventually leads to your financial freedom.

This is a very simple exercise. Take out your bank statements (both checking and savings accounts) and credit-card statements from the past month.

From the bank statements, do the following calculation on each one and add up the total:

**Closing balance – Opening balance
= Bank account cash flow**

From your credit-card statements, do the following calculation:

**New balance – Previous balance
= Debt spending**

Finally, calculate the following number:

**Bank account cash flow – Debt spending
= True last-month cash flow**

Here is an example of what this might look like:

Bank accounts			
	Closing balance	Opening balance	Difference
Checking 1	125.00	500.00	−375.00
Checking 2	384.02	662.08	−278.06
Savings 1	1,000.02	0.24	999.78
	Bank account cash flow		**346.72**

Credit cards			
	New balance	Previous balance	Difference
Credit Card	6,500.00	5,123.00	1,377.00
	Debt spending		1,377.00
	True last-month cash flow		**−1,030.28**

In this example, if you are looking only at your bank accounts and ignoring your credit card, you are missing the fact that you overspent by over $1,000 in the last month. This hidden growing debt is what keeps people from getting out of the struggling phase.

The true last-month cash-flow number is just a snapshot and may not give you the full picture of your finances, but it gives you a sense of which direction things are leaning. If you want to get an even better view, repeat the process for the last six months, and average the six numbers. This should give you an even clearer picture of what's going on.

The true last-month cash-flow number staring back at you is your *true* story, and it will line up with what you have been feeling in your gut about your money. Based on the "Analyze Your Cash Flow" section of this chapter, which level do you think you are on?

Chapter 5: **Spending Control**

BE SURE YOU KNOW THE CONDITION OF YOUR FLOCKS,
GIVE CAREFUL ATTENTION TO YOUR HERDS.

—Proverbs 27:23

IT'S NOT YOUR SALARY THAT MAKES YOU RICH,
IT'S YOUR SPENDING HABITS.

—Charles A. Jaffe (famous chess master)

Your Budget

To transform your financial situation and take full advantage of the Wealth Cycle, you need to use the right tools. The purpose of the next few chapters is to introduce you to the key tools that you have to employ throughout the Wealth Cycle, and to teach you how to use them effectively. The first area where you need a tool is spending control, to take control of the cash-flow equation so that the spending side comes down and you have more money available for your wealth-building activities. If you did the true last-month cash-flow calculation in the last chapter, you are starting to see where you may have spending control issues that need to be reined in.

The tool of choice for spending control is a budget.

I'm going to pause here and let you release all of the negative emotions you may have about budgeting. Take a deep breath and exhale slowly. Allow all those fears, frustrations, and concerns about budgeting to come rushing in, and then release them as you breathe out.

Did you do it? If not, I'll give you another moment to do so.

Done? Great!

Even if you still didn't take a moment to release your emotions about budgeting, there was a reason I included that small exercise. It is because the reason people struggle with budgeting has nothing to do with how complicated it is to create one. The reason people struggle with budgeting is because of the emotions that rise up when they take a realistic look at their spending and realize that they thought they were in a much better place than they actually are. To overcome these emotions around budgeting, you have to become very methodical and mechanical about the process.

For any of you who are sports fans, this analogy about budgeting might be helpful. When broken down to its simplest form, a budget is a *playbook*.

A coach in any team sport knows that going into a game without a game plan is a serious mistake. Coaches use their playbook as a written explanation of their approaches and strategies to defeat their opponent. Keeping the playbook in their head would not work, because our minds have a way of changing the way we remember things and giving us false information. In the heat of a game, even if they have all their plays memorized, coaches need the playbook to effectively communicate to their team what they need to do.

In your financial life, the coach is you, the players are your money, and the playbook is your budget. You use your playbook to tell your players what to do so that they can win. Without this critical communication, your players (your money) will not work together as a team, and some of them will even work against each other without realizing it.

This financial playbook helps you to think about what you are going to do with every single dollar that comes your way, before you have the money in your hands. This is important because when money comes into our hands, we have a way of inventing uses for that money on the fly without taking into consideration the impact on the rest of our plan. This is similar to players on a basketball team deciding to take the game into their own hands and take every shot, without realizing that by doing so, they are missing too many shots and helping the other team get more opportunities to score; plus, they are not looking around for any of their teammates who are open and might get better shots.

To take the playbook analogy even further, one of the most important things that coaches have to do when they get into a game is to make adjustments once they size up their opponent. This means that the playbook is not a rigid document that must be followed at all costs but rather a fluid plan that can be adjusted as the circumstances warrant. This is the same way you should see your budget—as a living document that you constantly revise as you develop new needs or learn new information.

Now that you understand that a budget is your playbook, how do you create one that you can use effectively?

Your Needs, Wants, and Wishes

Before we get into the details of how to structure your budget, it's important to do some upfront thinking about every dollar that you spend while taking emotion out of the process.

A lot of the spending issues that you may be dealing with have to do with impulsive spending or spending when you don't see the full picture, so in the latter part of this chapter, I will show you how to see that full picture. The full picture of the playbook helps you to think about all components of the game, your competitor's strengths and weaknesses, and the ways you can exploit what they're doing. It shows you how you can take charge of the situation against your opponent.

When it comes to money, your opponent is the things that take money out of your pocket. So when you are doing this initial exercise to scout your competition, it's important to learn as much as possible.

The most important thing to know about your opponent is that not all expenditures are equal; therefore you should not treat them all the same. There are three kinds of expenses that take money out of your pocket: needs, wants, and wishes.

- **Needs** are things that are critical to your survival. Examples of this are food, shelter, transportation, and, if you have kids, education.
- **Wants** are all those things that you think are needs but you could do without and still survive. For example, a big one in this category is cable. You do not need television to survive, but a lot of people think they do.
- **Wishes** are all those things that you really don't need, and either they are out of your reach right now financially or, if you really look closely, you're spending money on them but you shouldn't be, because they are extravagant.

The first thing to do is list out all of your expenses on a sheet of paper. Don't worry; the first time you do this, you're not going to write down everything, because there's a lot of spending you do that you don't necessarily think about. For people who are already solid, this is probably an exercise that you've done before, so you can skip this section. Later on I will show you my Money in Motion exercise, which applies to all levels when budgeting and will be more relevant to you.

For all those who are struggling and moving toward steady, once you list all of your expenses, the next thing to do is to put them into some sort of order in terms of needs, wants, and wishes according to the definitions above. This will start to show you what your spending priorities should be.

Be honest with yourself when you are going through this process. Put only essential items in the needs category, and be very diligent about putting things correctly in the wants and wishes categories even if you don't treat them like that today. For example, eating is a need, but eating at a restaurant is a want. And if you are struggling, eating at a restaurant is a wish until your financial situation is stabilized. The more honest you are during this process, the faster you will get to your goal.

If you are married, you should do this exercise with your spouse because you are two different people with different priorities, and those differing priorities can sometimes derail your plan.

The next thing to do for each of those items is figure the amount that you're spending on a monthly basis. As I said before, for anything that's not a recurring bill, you're probably going to get this part wrong because things such as food, clothes, and entertainment—all those types of things we tend to think we spend less on—are the ones that get us in trouble. So put down a number for each of the items as a starting point.

Remember the first part of the Wealth Cycle is Monitor. So once you have put a number next to each of these items, you should start paying attention to how much you actually spend on each of them.

Your Income

Once you record your estimated expenses, it's time to look at the income side of the equation. Most people think of their income as the annual money coming in, but this can be misleading because you are not taking into account all of the deductions to your paycheck before you actually get money to use. This is also true for small-business owners because they have to put aside money for taxes and expenses before spending on anything else. So it is important for you to figure out your net income rather than your gross income.

Then, if you are a Christian, that net income is still not the money you have available to spend. This is because 10 percent of your gross income is your tithe and not yours to keep. The tithe does not belong to your household but has to be returned to the house of the Lord, and then you work with the 90 percent remaining. The best way to take care of this is to calculate it as 10 percent of your prededuction income and make it the first item in your monthly budget.

To calculate your net monthly income, pull out your last pay stub and look at both the gross and the net number. Then do the following calculations based on whether you are paid weekly, twice a month, biweekly, or once a month:

Weekly

Monthly gross income = [Gross income on pay stub × 52] / 12

Monthly net income = [Net income on pay stub × 52] / 12

Monthly tithe = Monthly gross income × 10%

Amount available to spend = Monthly net income − Monthly tithe

Twice a month (e.g., day 15 and 31)

Monthly gross income = Gross income on pay stub × 2

Monthly net income = Net income on pay stub × 2

Monthly tithe = Monthly gross income × 10%

Amount available to spend = Monthly net income − Monthly tithe

Biweekly (every two weeks)

Monthly gross income = [Gross income on pay stub × 26] / 12

Monthly net income = [Net income on pay stub × 26] / 12

Monthly tithe = Monthly gross income × 10%

Amount available to spend = Monthly net income − Monthly tithe

Once a month

Monthly tithe = Gross income on pay stub × 10%

Amount available to spend = Net income on pay stub − Monthly tithe

For people who have more irregular income (e.g., freelancers or contractors), you need to estimate your monthly income based on your past six months' earnings and then calculate a buffer to help you meet your obligations in the low months, when you don't earn as much as other months.

Now that you have your income written down, it's time to take action and use two tools to create your budget:

- Money in Motion budget
- Monthly working budget

Take Action: Create Your Budget

I n the chapter about the Wealth Cycle, I introduced you to my Money in Motion tool, and now I am going to go deeper and show you how this relates to creating your budget with a focus on the following topics:

- Installment debt
- Monthly budget
- Prosperity dollars

Step 1: Enter Installment Debts

The purpose of this step is to give you a realistic picture of how debt actively affects your ability to build wealth. In the leftmost column, list all of your installment debts with their total balance amounts—what is still remaining for you to pay off the debt.

Here is an example with a few credit cards, a student loan, and a mortgage:

Table 2: Money in Motion—Installment Debts

Installment debt	Budget	Prosperity dollars
Store card $1,000		
Gas card $1,200		
Bank credit card $5,000		
Student loan $20,000		
Mortgage $450,000		

Next, add in how much you pay monthly for each of the debts. This goes in the Budget column:

Table 3: Money in Motion—Debt Payments

Installment debt	Budget	Prosperity dollars
Store card $1,000	**Monthly payment** $100	
Gas card $1,200	**Monthly payment** $150	
Bank credit card $5,000	**Monthly payment** $275	
Student loan $20,000	**Monthly payment** $300	
Mortgage $450,000	**Monthly payment** $3,800	

Next, for each installment debt, enter its contribution to your prosperity, or how much this monthly bill contributes to your ownership of assets. These are the types of installment debts that contribute to prosperity:

- **Mortgage.** If you owe less than the house is worth, your prosperity dollars are the equity you have in the house (house value minus mortgage).
- **Student loan.** This contributes to your prosperity dollars because being educated increases your ability to be successful in life. It does not have a direct measurable amount, so mark it with ++.
- **Car loan.** If you have had your car for a few years and owe less on the car than it is worth, the profit you would make if you sold the car is your prosperity dollars.
- **Other.** Any other loan that is secured by something you own where the value of what you own is greater than the loan contributes to your ownership of assets.

Here is how our example would look if our house were worth $500,000:

Table 4: Money in Motion—Home Equity

Installment debt	Budget	Prosperity dollars
Store card $1,000	**Monthly payment** $100	$0
Gas card $1,200	**Monthly payment** $150	$0
Bank credit card $5,000	**Monthly payment** $275	$0
Student loan $20,000	**Monthly payment** $300	++
Mortgage $450,000	**Monthly payment** $3,800	$50,000[5]

---

[5] $500,000 (home value) – $450,000 (mortgage balance) = $50,000 (equity)

This now gives you a clear picture of where your installment debt fits into your wealth-building picture. The more installment debts you have that contribute nothing to your prosperity dollars, the greater the chance that you are struggling to move forward financially, because you are spending money that is contributing nothing to ownership. These types of installment debts have to be eliminated as soon as possible to start turning your situation around. We will talk more specifically about this in the next chapter.

Step 2: Enter Your Monthly Budget

The next step in developing your budget is to enter all of your monthly expenses. In this section you have to be as comprehensive as possible and cover all the things you spend money on monthly in the three categories: needs, wants, wishes. Here is a budget guideline to get you started—start off by multiplying the minimum percentage in the range with your net income and only increase it if absolutely necessary for that budget item. Even when increasing, make sure it doesn't go over the maximum percentage:

Table 5: Monthly Budget Guidelines

Category	Min %	Max %
Tithing[6]	10	10
Giving	5	50
Investing	10	30
Housing	20	40
Food	8	15
Transportation	8	15
Insurance	3	8
Medical/dental	4	8
Debt	0	10
Entertainment/recreation/clothing	4	10
School/childcare	0	10

[6] Unlike with other budget categories, the 10% is calculated off the gross income

In addition to these items, which are recurring amounts on a monthly basis, make sure to take into account irregular expenses and calculate a monthly amount to put away for them. Do this by figuring out your annual cost for the item and dividing by twelve. Here are some examples of irregular items:

- Taxes
- Home maintenance/improvement
- Vacation
- Holidays
- Gifts

So in our example, the budget would now look like this:

Table 6: Money in Motion—With Monthly Budget

Installment debt	Budget	Prosperity dollars
Store card $1,000	**Monthly payment** $100	$0
Gas card $1,200	**Monthly payment** $150	$0
Bank credit card $8,000	**Monthly payment** $275	$0
Student loan $20,000	**Monthly payment** $300	++
Mortgage $450,000	**Monthly payment** $3,800	$50,000
	Tithe $600	
	Utilities $175	
	Transportation $80	
	Childcare $1,200	
	Education $500	
	Food $900	
	...	

I'm not going to list everything here, because everybody and every household has a different budget. The main point is to list everything so that you see it all written down.

Step 3: List Your Prosperity Dollars

The final step is to list out your prosperity dollars in the right-hand column. In our example, we have already listed out the equity in our house in the prosperity column, so here are some additional items that go in that column:[7]

- **Tithing.** Similar to your student loan, you allocate this with ++ because it contributes to your prosperity, but there isn't a specific number to calculate.

- **Brokerage accounts.** Any investment accounts you hold should be listed with their most recent balances.

- **Retirement accounts (401(k)/403(b)/IRA/SEP).** You should be putting money into these types of accounts on a monthly basis because retirement has to be saved for over time.

- **Education (529 plan).** If you have kids, you should save for their college expenses in this type of account at a minimum.

---

[7] Go to www.yourwealthcycle.com/budget for a more comprehensive list of prosperity-dollar items and their explanations.

Our example now looks like this:

Table 7: Money in Motion—Prosperity Dollars

Installment debt	Budget	Prosperity dollars
Store card $1,000	**Monthly payment** $100	$0
Gas card $1,200	**Monthly payment** $150	$0
Bank credit card $8,000	**Monthly payment** $275	$0
Student loan $20,000	**Monthly payment** $300	++
Mortgage $450,000	**Monthly payment** $3,800	$50,000
	Tithe $600	++
	Utilities $175	$0
	Transportation $80	$0
	Childcare $1,200	$0
	Education $500	$0
	Food $900	$0
	...	$0
		401(k) $70,000
		529 plan $10,000

Step 4: Analyze Your Current Situation

Now that you have filled out your Money in Motion budget, it's time to determine what it all means. Typically, when I first do this exercise with my clients, there are three main patterns that may emerge.

Pattern 1

Installment debt	Budget	Prosperity dollars
A lot	Large	Very little

- A *lot of debt* in the first column
- A *large budget* in the second column because of their debt burden
- And *very little in prosperity dollars* in the third column because they are spending all the money on debt

Notice the word that is repeated in all three of those sentences: **debt.**

Pattern 2

Installment debt	Budget	Prosperity dollars
Minimal	Very large	Low

- Minimal debt
- *Large budget* with lots of wants and wishes
- *Low prosperity dollars* because the money is spent on non-essentials (wants and wishes) that don't contribute to wealth building

Pattern 3

Once in a while we get clients who have a Money in Motion budget that is very close to the ideal that we want everybody who is a serious wealth builder to have.

Installment debt	Budget	Prosperity dollars
Low/none	Low/modest	Large

- Low to no debt
- Low to modest budget
- Large prosperity dollars

Look at your own Money in Motion budget. Which of these patterns emerges for you? If your budget is close to the first pattern, you are most likely in the struggling or steady levels. If you are in the second pattern, chances are you believe you are solid, but you are more like a strong steady and are probably a life event away from dropping down into struggling. If you are in the last pattern, you are already somewhere between surplus and service.

Step 5: Determine Your Game Plan

After analyzing your current situation and determining what pattern you are displaying, you have a good sense of what you need to do to improve your situation. The steps are the same for everyone:

1. Pay off debt and/or lower your spending to free up money.

2. Apply the freed-up money and any additional income you can earn toward spending that is conducive to building wealth (prosperity dollars).

3. Repeat.

Let me show you how powerful this process is using the Money in Motion budget we used in our example and an alternative way one of the budget items could have worked.

In our example, we have the following budget item:

Installment debt	Budget	Prosperity dollars
Mortgage $450,000	**Monthly payment** $3,800	$50,000

The property in this example is most likely a single-family home, so we are responsible for the whole amount of the mortgage payment and don't earn any income by owning the property. Now imagine if we instead had purchased a three-family unit where each tenant pays us $2,300 per month. The budget item would now look like this:

Installment debt	Budget	Prosperity dollars
Mortgage $450,000	**Monthly payment** $3,800 **Monthly rental income** $4,600 **Positive cash flow** $4,600 – $3,800 = **$800**	$50,000

Just by making a different decision about what type of home to purchase, we maintain the same prosperity dollars for equity, but we now have a positive number in our budget that can actually help our prosperity dollars to grow. We could invest that money, pay down debt, or even pay off the mortgage faster so that our prosperity dollars for this budget item goes up to $500,000.

With the paid-off property, the budget item looks like this:

Installment debt	Budget	Prosperity dollars
Mortgage $0	**Monthly payment** $0 **Monthly rental income** $4,600 **Positive cash flow** $4,600	$500,000

The prosperity dollars are now the full value of the property because there is no debt on it, AND we are earning money from the asset every month.

Do you see the power of focusing your budget toward prosperity dollars? I get excited every time I show examples like this because you don't have to be a genius to change your thinking about how you spend money; you just have to clearly see how it all comes together to create your wealth machine.

So with the knowledge of how powerful your decisions about how your money is distributed can be, go on to the last step.

Step 6: Create Your Working Monthly Budget

The Money in Motion budget is a planning tool used to help you nail down your strategy for your money. Based on what you have learned about where you need to focus your attention to build wealth, you can now go back and create a working monthly budget that aligns with your Money in Motion strategy.

The working monthly budget has two components: income and expenses. As mentioned earlier in this chapter, the income you should list on this budget is your net income, because this is the money you actually have to work with.

Here is an example of a simple working monthly budget for somebody who makes $80,000/year but is struggling:[8]

Table 8: Working Monthly Budget—Struggling

Category	Amount	%
INCOME		
Net income: salary	$3,500	88
Net income: commissions	$500	13
Total net income	**$4,000**	100
EXPENSES		
Needs		
Tithing	$667[9]	17
Giving	$20	1
Investing	—	0
Housing and utilities	$1,200	30
Food	$480	12
Car payment	$500	13
Kids' education	$500	13
Cell phone	$300	8
Insurance	$200	5
Medical/dental	$200	5
Debt	$590	15
Wants		
Dining out	$1,000	25
Cable	$200	5
Wishes	—	
TOTAL EXPENSES	**$5,857**	**146**
TOTAL CASH FLOW	**($1,857)**	

---

[8] For examples of monthly working budgets for all five levels, go to http://www.yourwealthcycle.com/budget.

[9] You may have noticed that this number is not 10 percent of the income number above. That is because the tithe is calculated using the gross income, while the budget uses the net income.

To increase your effectiveness, go back to the exercise you did in the "Your Needs, Wants, and Wishes" section of this chapter, and look at all the items in your budget. For people who are struggling, you may do this exercise and realize, as in the example above, that there is not enough income to cover all the expenses you have listed. The first thing you should do is eliminate all the wants and wishes from your budget. You should be operating on the lowest possible expenses you need to survive, so any expenses that are not absolutely necessary are bad stewardship on your part.

For the example above, we might make the following adjustments:

- Stop eating out.
- Cut off cable.
- Get a cheaper cell-phone plan.
- Start using coupons at the grocery store to get the food bill down.
- Shop for cheaper insurance.
- Put the central air system on a timer so it's not running all the time, and save on utilities.

With all those changes, our new budget might look like this:

Table 9: Working Monthly Budget—Struggling (with Adjustments)

Category	Amount	%
INCOME		
Net income: salary	$3,500	88
Net income: commissions	$500	13
Total net income	**$4,000**	100
EXPENSES		
Needs		
Tithing	$667	17
Giving	$20	1
Investing	—	0
Housing and utilities	$1,000	25
Food	$350	9
Car payment	$500	13
Kids' education	$500	13
Cell phone	$150	4
Insurance	$150	4
Medical/dental	$200	5
Debt	$590	15
Wants		
Dining out	—	0
Cable	—	0
Wishes	—	
		0
TOTAL EXPENSES	**$4,127**	**103**
TOTAL CASH FLOW	**($127)**	

Rather than a deficit of over $1,800 every month, we now have just over $100 in negative cash flow, which is a lot more manageable.

If you eliminate all your wants and wishes, but the numbers still don't work, you have to make some major lifestyle changes. This may mean taking on a second job, or it may mean downsizing where you live or what you drive. Aggressively take whatever action you need to take until the numbers work out. You will find yourself much more focused and disciplined about this process if you review your Money in Motion budget often (at least monthly) so you know why these short-term sacrifices move you faster toward your long-term goals.

If you are solid or surplus, the focus of your working monthly budget is to make sure that you are growing your prosperity-dollar allocations. So you may also make some short-term sacrifices if you want to accelerate your wealth-building efforts but for a different reason. You probably also have more wants included in the budget—but make sure they are not impeding your ability to increase prosperity dollars.

People at the service level should also operate with a working monthly budget, because stewardship of your money is still important at that level. Even when professional musicians are at the peak of their career, they still spend time practicing the fundamentals that got them to where they are, and the same should be true about managing your money. The main difference between the other levels and service is that your budget can have much broader categories, and wishes are a big part of what you include.

Finally, make sure to monitor on a daily basis. The working monthly budget should be used together with whatever system you feel most comfortable to track how you are spending your money. I call this your ledger. Some people prefer a handwritten version, and others prefer to use software. The important thing is that you use something to keep you accountable to following the guidelines in your working monthly budget.

As you track yourself against the budget, you should constantly look for opportunities to get out of monthly obligations that are not serving to increase your prosperity dollars, and to lower your required expenses on items. This process is really what is at the heart of the Monitor and Analyze steps of the Wealth Cycle, and you never stop doing them. You use the tracking of your working monthly budget to monitor, and then you use your Money in Motion budget to analyze your cash flow. If you stopped at monitoring and analyzing, you would become very good at managing your money, but you would not be building wealth. That's why it is important to work on the Increase component to make your money grow. The next two chapters are dedicated to three key components of the Increase strategy: debt elimination, saving, and investing.

If you still have installment debt, the area where you have the most dramatic impact on your ability to increase cash flow is debt elimination. So this topic is the sole focus of the next chapter. Read on to learn about my system for helping people get out of debt.

Chapter 6:   # Debt Elimination

OWE NOTHING TO ANYONE EXCEPT TO LOVE ONE
ANOTHER; FOR HE WHO LOVES HIS NEIGHBOR HAS
FULFILLED THE LAW.

—Romans 13:28

IT IS THE DEBTOR THAT IS RUINED BY HARD TIMES.

—Rutherford B. Hayes

Debt Is Slavery

At the beginning of this book, I spoke about the bumper sticker that said, "I owe, I owe, it's off to work I go." I said this tongue in cheek, but the issue of debt and people struggling under the bondage of debt is a very serious one. When I do trainings about debt, I often refer to it as a form of slavery, which I know is a harsh term to use and one that conjures up a lot of emotions—but if you set aside the historical weight of that word for a moment and consider one of the definitions in the *Webster Dictionary* of "slave," you will understand what I mean: "one that is completely subservient to a dominating influence." This is exactly how I see the power of debt play out in people's lives. Debt is a dominating influence because it significantly limits the choices you can make with your money. You are subservient to the force because every month, when you get paid, you have no choice but to send the money you owe to your creditors. If you feel strongly that this is not the case, go a few months without paying your mortgage and see what happens. The Bible says in Proverbs 22:7: "the borrower is slave to the lender."

If you are a person of integrity, defaulting on your debts when you have the ability to pay them is not an option, because this is equivalent to breaking a covenant that you made with the lender. Therefore, all lenders you owe money to are your masters, whether you agree with this or not, because they have a right to your property (money) until the debt is paid off.

Consider these five characteristics of debt slavery:

1. You are making someone else rich from the sweat of your brow.
2. You have a feeling that you will always be paying off debts.
3. You have low financial intellect, and financial freedom eludes you because you're not aware of the alternatives.
4. You are in bondage because you have no money and you cannot do what you want to do when you want to do it.
5. You work all your life, but you have no financial legacy to show for it.

When you read each of these characteristics, does it make you jump with joy? Of course not. There is nothing edifying about living in debt—and yet people blindly live their lives as if there were no alternative, because we have all been conditioned from a very young age to feel entitled to stuff even if it is not within our means to get it. And getting a loan is advertised as if it were a virtue, rather than something to be avoided. It is big business for banks to make money off you with the interest you pay on your debt, so the positive marketing messages about it are not going away anytime soon.

Debt Is Expensive

Debt is also more expensive than you may imagine. When I speak with people about building wealth, they invariably tell me that they can't afford to invest. I usually respond to this by telling them that they are already investing in the very expensive vehicle of debt. For example, let's compare paying off a $5,000 credit card with a 10 percent interest rate (and I am being generous) versus investing in a mutual fund with a starting principal of $5,000 and a return of 10 percent. In each instance, let's say you pay $100 every month. It will take you just over five years to pay off that credit card, and you will pay $1,495 in interest over the period, whereas the mutual fund would have grown to $15,230 in five years.

This is how both scenarios look compared against each other:

Table 10: Cost of Debt vs. Investing in Mutual Fund

Scenario	Paying off $5,000	Investing in a mutual fund
Initial Balance	$5,000	$0
Interest Rate/ Rate of Return	10%	10%
Monthly investment	$107	$107
Comparison period	60 months to pay off	60 months of steady investment
Total investment	$5,000 (principal) + $1,342 (interest) = **$6,342**	[$107 × 60 months] = **$6,420**
Asset value at end	$0	**$8,623**
Total prosperity dollars earned	$0	$8,623 − $6,420 = **$2,203**

So for an investment of roughly $6,400 over five years, your investment in debt brings you back to ground zero, whereas your investment in the mutual fund leaves you with an asset worth over $8,500.

This becomes even worse when you are carrying more debt. Consider this example where the total credit card debt is $25,000:

Table 11: Cost of Debt vs. Investing in Mutual Fund (Larger Debt)

Scenario	Paying off $25,000	Investing in a mutual fund
Initial Balance	$25,000	$0
Interest Rate/ Rate of Return	10%	10%
Monthly investment	$531	$531
Comparison period	60 months to pay off	60 months of steady investment
Total investment	$25,000 (principal) + $4,469 (interest) = **$ 29,469**	[$531 × 60 months] = $ 31,860
Asset value at end	$0	**$ 40,978**
Total prosperity dollars earned	$0	$40,978 – $31,860= **$9,118**

At the end of this scenario, you are comparing starting at zero vs. having an asset worth over $40,000.

Can you see why I say debt is expensive?

Now, if you are struggling with debt and think that you are in the minority, don't be fooled. There are plenty of people who are well dressed, driving a nice car, and living in a nice house who are in just as much debt slavery as you. Their numbers are just bigger. They may smile and look good on the outside, but on the inside they're slowly dying because they have no idea how to get out of the bondage—just like you.

Fortunately, you had the wisdom to seek help by picking up this book, so I am going to share with you just as I do in my live trainings and seminars—without pulling any punches. I think debt is a topic that you cannot tiptoe around; you just have to face it head on and accept that it is a problem.

Over the years, I've developed a very simple system that is similar to a lot of the systems that you see out there related to paying down debt. Don't let the simplicity fool you, though. As I mentioned before, it is not the mechanics of finances that trips people up; it is their emotions and habits about money that do them in. If you follow these steps and stay consistent and disciplined, you will get out of debt and free yourself from the shackles of slavery. Doing so will also exponentially accelerate your ability to build wealth.

The Four Rules to Get Out of Debt

There are four rules to get out of debt. These four rules are the foundation of my tool for getting you out of debt, the Debt Eliminator:

1. Stop spending.
2. Pay the minimum on all cards except one.
3. Establish a debt multiplier of at least a hundred dollars.
4. Stay disciplined.

Don't let the simple-sounding nature of these rules make you discount the power of the process. If you diligently follow all four rules and integrate them into your life, you will see a tremendous turnaround in your financial situation.

"Stop spending" is simply another way of telling you to be disciplined about the budget you set up in the previous chapter. Don't add any new debt to your credit cards. In fact, make it a policy to pay for everything with cash or a debit card. Follow your playbook and adjust as things change, but don't trick yourself into thinking you can become less diligent when you start experiencing some success with the process.

Sometimes when I tell people to pay the minimum on all cards but one, they respond by saying that they pay more than the minimum on all their cards, and they think that is helping their situation. Don't fall into that trap. Paying a little bit extra on several debts and paying a lot on one debt while keeping everything else at the minimum have two drastically different outcomes. The "little bit on each card" strategy does not work, and I will show you why the strategy I teach is so powerful when I go into more detail about the Debt Eliminator.

Establishing a debt multiplier of at least one hundred dollars means that you find an extra one hundred dollars in your budget to overpay the first debt that you are going to focus on.

Finally, staying disciplined is critical to your success. Depending on how many installment debts you have, your debt-elimination process may span several years, and you have to make sure that you stay the course, because the benefits at the end of your debt-elimination journey are abundant.

Create Your Debt Eliminator

So how do you actually set up the Debt Eliminator? There are three steps in the process.

Step 1: List All of Your Debts

List all of your debts in order of size from smallest to largest using the Debt Eliminator table. Include every creditor, the monthly payment, the outstanding balance, and the interest rate. Here is an example with all the debt information filled out. This example uses rounded numbers for simplicity, but make sure to use exact numbers for your own debts:

Table 12: Debt Eliminator—List All Debts

Debt	Min. monthly payment	Balance	Interest rate	Debt Eliminator	Priority	Time
Dept. store card #1	$15	$275	18%			
Dept. store card #2	$25	$500	18%			
Dept. store card #3	$40	$1,200	18%			
Major credit card #1	$45	$1,500	18%			
Major credit card #2	$90	$3,000	18%			
Major credit card #3	$125	$4,200	18%			
Car loan	$275	$11,000	12%			
Student loan	$250	$20,000	6%			
Mortgage	$1,000	$150,000	7%			
Total	$1,865	$191,675				

Step 2: Decide on the Size of Your Debt Multiplier

The next step is to decide how much you can budget monthly toward paying down your debt. This number has to be over and above what you currently pay on the minimum balances. I call this your debt multiplier and suggest that it should be at least one hundred dollars, but the larger you can make it, the faster you will pay down your debt.

Step 3: Turn Your Debt Multiplier into a Debt Eliminator

This step is where the magic happens. You will continue paying the minimum payment on all your cards except the one with the lowest outstanding balance. For that card, you will add $100 to the minimum payment and accelerate how quickly you pay it off. So in our example from the previous step, the payment to the first debt in the list would go from $15/month to $115/month. This is your Debt Eliminator. Because the outstanding balance is $275, it will take about three months to completely pay off (eliminate) that card. This takes into account any interest payments that you will pay during that time.

Getting that first card paid off feels like a great accomplishment, especially if you have been struggling for a long time. To keep the momentum of this first achievement, two things are extremely important:

1. Make sure to keep up with the other minimum monthly payments.
2. Do *not* (and this is perhaps the most important thing) incur any additional debt.

Instead, maintain your discipline, and once the first card is paid off, take the total amount you were paying on the first card, $115 (minimum payment + debt multiplier), and create a new Debt Eliminator by adding it to the minimum payment for the second debt. This Debt Eliminator of $140 will get rid of the second card with a balance of $500 in another three months, so in our sixth months, we have paid off two debts.

Repeat this process until all of the installment debt is eliminated. Here is how the completed table looks for our example.

Table 13: Debt Eliminator—List All Debts (Complete)

Debt	Min. monthly payment	Balance	Interest rate (%)	Debt Eliminator	Priority	Time (months)
Dept. store card #1	$15	$275	18	$115	1	3
Dept. store card #2	$25	$500	18	$140	2	6
Dept. store card #3	$40	$1,200	18	$180	3	12
Major credit card #1	$45	$1,500	18	$225	4	18
Major credit card #2	$90	$3,000	18	$315	5	25
Major credit card #3	$125	$4,200	18	$440	6	31
Car loan	$275	$11,000	12	$715	7	38
Student loan	$250	$20,000	6	$965	8	53
Mortgage	$1,000	$150,000	7	$1,965	9	147
Total	**$1,865**	**$191,675**				**147**

Using this structured Debt Eliminator method, we are able to pay off **all** of our debt, including our mortgage, in 147 months, or approximately twelve years. This is a powerful outcome for starting out with a debt multiplier of just a hundred dollars a month!

Table 14 shows a snapshot of a few months during the process so you can really understand how this works.[10] The Debt Eliminator in each month is highlighted in bold.

Do you see how the Debt Eliminator gets to work on a debt and destroys it for you? Especially later on in the process, when it has grown in size. I hope you can see how superior this method is to sending a few extra dollars a month to each of the cards instead of focusing on one at a time.

Now, as I mentioned before, the key for all of this to be successful is to completely avoid adding any new debt. You have to live within your means throughout the process, or you will sabotage yourself. Of course, life events happen that may momentarily take you off course, but if you train yourself to focus on the end result, you can achieve this significant objective.

Look back at the example table, and you will notice that there is an added bonus at the end of this whole process. We now have an additional $1,965 a month to spend toward building up our prosperity dollars.

Before I close this chapter, there are two additional illustrations of the Debt Eliminator that I would like to show you. The first is the power of increasing the size of your debt multiplier. Instead of shooting for the minimum hundred dollars that I recommend, you should try to get your debt multiplier as high as possible right from the beginning because you will get out of debt faster.

---

[10] If you need help generating your own Debt Eliminator, go to http://www.yourwealthcycle/debt-eliminator and use our free calculator to do the math for you and show you how soon you can get out of debt with the process.

Table 14: Debt Eliminator—Illustration

Name of debt	Begin bal. / payment	Month 4 bal. / payment	Month 7 bal. / payment	Month 14 bal. / payment	Month 19 bal. / payment	Month 26 bal. / payment	Month 32 bal. / payment	Month 39 bal. / payment
Dept. store card #1	$275 / **$115**	$0	$0	$0	$0	$0	$0	$0
Dept. store card #2	$500 / $25	$425 / **$140**	$0	$0	$0	$0	$0	$0
Dept. store card #3	$1,200 / $40	$1,100 / $40	$874 / **$180**	$0	$0	$0	$0	$0
Major credit card #1	$1,500 / $45	$1,408 / $45	$1,335 / $45	$804 / **$225**	$0	$0	$0	$0
Major credit card #2	$3,000 / $90	$2,816 / $90	$2,670 / $90	$2,305 / $90	$1,726 / **$315**	$0	$0	$0
Major credit card #3	$4,200 / $125	$3,946 / $125	$3,746 / $125	$3,242 / $125	$2,849 / $125	$1,855 / **$440**	$0	$0
Car loan	$11,000 / $275	$10,330 / $275	$9,810 / $275	$8,534 / $275	$7,566 / $275	$6,128 / $275	$4,102 / **$715**	$0
Student Loan	$20,000 / $250	$19,396 / $250	$18,934 / $250	$17,830 / $250	$17,018 / $250	$15,846 / $250	$14,809 / $250	$12,799 / **$965**
Mortgage	$150,000 / $1,000	$149,496 / $1,000	$149,110 / $1,000	$148,182 / $1,000	$147,496 / $1,000	$146,502 / $1,000	$145,616 / $1,000	$144,544 / $1,000

Here is the same borrower I used in the previous example, but this time we are using a $500 debt multiplier:

Table 15: Debt Eliminator—Larger Multiplier Example

Debt	Min. monthly payment	Balance	Interest rate (%)	Debt Eliminator	Priority	Time (months)
Dept. store card #1	$15	$275	18	$515	1	1
Dept. store card #2	$25	$500	18	$540	2	2
Dept. store card #3	$40	$1,200	18	$580	3	4
Major credit card #1	$45	$1,500	18	$625	4	6
Major credit card #2	$90	$3,000	18	$715	5	10
Major credit card #3	$125	$4,200	18	$840	6	15
Car loan	$275	$11,000	12	$1,115	7	23
Student loan	$250	$20,000	6	$1,365	8	35
Mortgage	$1,000	$150,000	7	$2,365	9	111
Total	**$1,865**	**$191,675**				**111**

By changing the debt multiplier to $500, we get out of debt in 111 months instead of 147 months—36 months or three years earlier. So instead of paying off all our debt, including mortgage, in twelve years, we pay it off in nine years. It's definitely worth it to make your debt multiplier as high as possible.

The second illustration is for areas of the country that have a higher cost of living. I live in Los Angeles, and things are much more expensive here than where my father lives in Minnesota. With a debt multiplier of a hundred dollars, it would take people here a lot longer to pay off their debts. The same is true for other high-cost areas, such as New York. The reason is both the cost of living is higher and so monthly expenses are higher, but also people in these areas who are struggling tend to have much higher levels of debt.

Here is a sample LA Debt Eliminator:

Table 16: Debt Eliminator—"Los Angeles Debt" Example

Debt	Min. monthly payment	Balance	Interest rate (%)	Debt Eliminator	Priority	Time (months)
Dept. store card #1	$15	$500	18	$615	1	1
Dept. store card #2	$40	$1,200	18	$655	2	3
Dept. store card #3	$150	$5,000	18	$805	3	9
Major credit card #1	$210	$7,000	18	$1,105	4	15
Major credit card #2	$330	$11,000	18	$1,345	5	22
Major credit card #3	$510	$17,000	18	$1,855	6	28
Car loan	$1,170	$55,000	9	$3,025	7	39
Second mortgage	$630	$105,000	6	$3,655	8	69
Mortgage	$3,366	$550,000	7	$7,315	9	159
Total	**$6,715**	**$191,675**				**159**

We start with a $600 debt multiplier, but it still takes a longer time to pay off all our debt than in our original example. Can you imagine if we contributed only $100 a month to the multiplier?

So if you live in one of the higher-cost areas of the country, make sure to use a larger debt multiplier that is in line with your cost of living and debt balances.

Now that you understand how the Debt Eliminator works, don't just do the exercise on paper and then frame it and put it up on the wall. Do the calculations, and get started as soon as possible! If you think you don't have enough to get started, sell everything you haven't worn in the last ninety days and pay off your lowest card balance so you can use what you are paying on that card as your debt multiplier, because it is prosperity and get-out-of-debt time!

Chapter 7:

SaVesting

THEN THE MAN WHO HAD RECEIVED ONE BAG OF GOLD CAME.
"MASTER," HE SAID, "I KNEW THAT YOU ARE A HARD MAN,
HARVESTING WHERE YOU HAVE NOT SOWN AND GATHERING
WHERE YOU HAVE NOT SCATTERED SEED. SO I WAS AFRAID
AND WENT OUT AND HID YOUR GOLD IN THE GROUND.
SEE, HERE IS WHAT BELONGS TO YOU."

HIS MASTER REPLIED, "YOU WICKED, LAZY SERVANT! SO YOU KNEW
THAT I HARVEST WHERE I HAVE NOT SOWN AND GATHER WHERE
I HAVE NOT SCATTERED SEED? WELL THEN, YOU SHOULD HAVE
PUT MY MONEY ON DEPOSIT WITH THE BANKERS, SO THAT WHEN
I RETURNED I WOULD HAVE RECEIVED IT BACK WITH INTEREST.

"SO TAKE THE BAG OF GOLD FROM HIM AND GIVE IT TO THE ONE
WHO HAS TEN BAGS. FOR WHOEVER HAS WILL BE GIVEN MORE,
AND THEY WILL HAVE AN ABUNDANCE. WHOEVER DOES NOT HAVE,
EVEN WHAT THEY HAVE WILL BE TAKEN FROM THEM."

—Matthew 25:24–29

One of the things you might have realized so far in this book is that personal finance is not complicated. In fact, nothing is too complex in this book for somebody with more than a seventh-grade education to understand. What is challenging for most people is actually taking action on the things they need to do to change their financial situation. This is why when I travel around the world to teach about personal finance and wealth building, I focus heavily on the practical aspects and how to get into motion as soon as possible.

It's very simple for you to understand that you need to have a budget and that you need to get out of debt, but the amount of changes in behavior that need to happen for you to realize these goals is where the difficulty lies. Most personal-finance gurus cover both budgeting and debt elimination in great length, so there is nothing new to teach there.

There is one area, though, where I believe I have a different philosophy from a lot of personal-finance trainers that I have followed over the years. This has to do with the way that you sequence your savings and investing goals when you are moving through struggling to solid and surplus. There is a philosophy you may have heard taught that you should focus all of your initial financial strategy on getting out of debt and limit your saving to building up an emergency fund. In this approach, you should defer investing until you have eliminated your debt, because the conventional wisdom is that debt earns a negative interest rate and works against any gains you would get investing.

I strongly disagree with this approach. I believe in what I call SaVesting, where you work on all three areas simultaneously. You work on eliminating your debt while putting away money in savings *and* starting to get involved in some basic investing. The reason is that if you spend all your time paying down your debt, and it takes you five years to do so, at the end of that time, all you will have is zero—you will not be able to recapture the time you lost to take advantage of compound interest. In contrast, if you spend the five years (or maybe it takes you a little bit longer, six years) to pay down debt, and at the same time you invest some portion of the money, you will not only come out of the situation with zero debt but will also have already started the process of building assets and will have a positive net worth. This is a better position to be in than people who look up after five years and find their net worth is exactly zero.

I am so passionate about this approach because the most important factor you are working against in your financial life is time. The longer you defer becoming an investor, the longer it will take for you to flip the switch and become a wealth builder. So in this chapter, I focus on teaching you some practical lessons on how to become a SaVestor. The chapter is broken up into two parts that separate the saving and investing portions, but your goals should be to work on both areas at the same time and incorporate both strategies into your financial plan.

So future SaVestors, let's start by talking about saving like a pro.

Saving like a Pro

THE PLANS OF THE DILIGENT LEAD TO PROFIT AS SURELY AS HASTE LEADS TO POVERTY.

—Proverbs 21:5

When you are struggling or steady, you need to give yourself room to breathe in order to start improving your financial situation. If there isn't an immediate opportunity to get promoted or take on a second job, the best way to do this is to do better on the spending side of the equation. One of the best ways to become a master of your cash flow is to become one of the best savers you know. This is what I call saving like a pro. It takes the concept of getting a good deal while spending the least amount possible and turns it up several notches. People around you will think you are cheap, but the difference between being cheap and saving like a pro is that with this approach, you still care about quality, so the objective is not always to get the lowest price. The objective is to get the best value for your money.

Ninety-Five Strategies to Help You Save Money

I've organized this section of the book by beginner, intermediate, and advanced because the concept of saving is different depending on how experienced you are already with making smart money decisions. Those who are struggling are most likely not going to save on their investment portfolio, because they most likely don't have one!

You will notice that the advanced-strategies section is quite light. I am assuming that by the time you are advanced, you will start coming up with your own ideas on how to more efficiently use your money. That's when it gets really fun—when you start seeing these things for yourself.

There are three sections in each area:

Low-hanging fruit. Most of the items in this section are things you can take action on immediately and experience savings within a month or two.

Extra effort. These items require more effort, and the savings realized take more time but are very much worth it eventually.

Mind-set. The items in these sections are not actions but ways of thinking that are critical to you becoming a savings pro.

You can treat each list as a financial to-do list and work through each of the suggestions. If you already do something that I am suggesting, check it off and move on to the next one. The idea is to implement as many of the recommendations as possible.

Beginner Strategies

▶ *Low-Hanging Fruit*

1. If you are struggling financially, cancel your cable and get a library card. Television does nothing for your bank account or financial well-being. You can watch enough programming by streaming on your mobile devices to give you just as much entertainment for a fraction of the price. Besides, how many of the hundreds of channels you pay for do you actually watch?
2. Call all creditors and ask for a lower rate.
3. Examine your monthly bills for overcharges to be removed. Then call your creditors and point them out. It may result in a credit.
4. Use a gallon jug or large container and call it a Prosperity Jar and start saving your loose change. Put extra cash in it, and you'll be surprised how much money you can accumulate.
5. Carry a tip card or download a tip-calculator app on your phone. Then when you are at a restaurant, calculate the correct tip before adding it to the bill. Rather than being embarrassed, many people leave a larger tip than necessary.
6. Give yourself an allowance and do not spend haphazardly, using the ATM like a piggy bank. Discipline yourself and live off of your allowance.
7. Do not leave every light on when you are at home. If you had to put a dime in the light switch to turn on the lights or a quarter to watch TV, you would be more careful with how you used your utilities.

8. Unplug the extra refrigerator. You will be amazed at how much electricity you can save.

9. Recycle if you are in a state where you get a deposit for your bottles. Otherwise you are throwing money away.

10. Talk is cheap. Reduce your phone bill by changing to an inexpensive carrier. Whenever possible, use the Internet. It is less expensive to send e-mails to your friends and family than to call them.

11. Never go shopping hungry. Your empty stomach will cause you to buy 10 percent more food than you had originally intended.

12. Buy generic or store brands whenever possible.

13. Carry a small calculator when shopping. Check and compare unit prices.

14. Take a few moments to put together a grocery list, and stick to it. Avoid impulse buying!

15. Always shop with coupons. Some grocery stores give double value for coupons. However, avoid the habit of buying things just because you have a coupon. Many items end up in the trash.

16. Don't buy lottery tickets even if they seem like a minimal purchase. You can end up spending hundreds of dollars on lottery tickets each year and recoup only a five-dollar win. Look at the chances of your winning versus the money spent, risk versus reward. You actually have two chances of winning: slim and none!

17. Cancel subscriptions to magazines. Buy your favorite magazines individually only when you are sure that you will have the time to read them. Otherwise, you are paying to accumulate unread stacks of paper.

18. Bring your lunch and snacks to work. If you spend $10 a day on lunch, five times per week, that's $50 per week. Multi-

ply that by fifty-two weeks a year, and you will have spent $2,600 a year.

19. Review your medical bill and ask questions. Some medical bills have errors.

20. Take advantage of your employee benefit plans. Most people are not aware of the benefits provided through their company, so do some research today and find out all the ways you can save because you work where you work. Benefits can be for things as varied as subscriptions, optical examinations, movie tickets, and even access to discounts for legal advice.

▶ *Extra Effort*

21. Avoid dating people with no money. If they're broke while you're dating them, they're displaying their budgeting habits. Remember that there's a difference between someone who is young and struggling to get ahead and someone who is consistently broke.

22. Get a second job, your debt job, whose income will be used solely to pay off debt—for example, answering service operator; kitty chauffeur; dog, plant, or house sitter; house cleaner; or personal shopper.

23. Go on a game show to earn extra cash.

24. If you tithe or give money to the church, secure the proper statement from the church to verify the amount. If you itemize when preparing your tax return, the government will give you a deduction and you will lower your taxable income.

25. Limit the number of credit cards in your name. I believe two is enough, one personal and one business. However, all of them should be paid off at the end of the month.

26. Talk to a financial advisor before settling on an insurance policy. Then try to pay yearly or every six months. You can

usually get a discount if you pay the full premium rather than monthly installments.

27. Adjust your thermostat when you're away from home for long periods of time. My mother used to say, "Don't heat up the furniture!" (I grew up in Minnesota.) The same holds true for your air conditioner. Do not pay to keep the walls cool.

28. Install a climate-control device. Some of these devices will turn on your air conditioner or heater fifteen minutes before you get home rather than running all day.

29. Use personal heaters or fans when your entire house is not occupied.

30. If you live by yourself, take in a reliable roommate. Share the cost and utilize your surplus cash to pay off debt.

31. Purchase a used car. New cars have higher monthly payments, and the car itself decreases in value. Used-car purchases also save on insurance premiums. You get lower rates on used cars.

32. Routine upkeep on your vehicle will save you from spending lump sums of money when the car breaks down from lack of maintenance.

33. Drive your car carefully. It will keep you from paying outrageous amounts on speeding tickets and increase the longevity of your brakes.

34. Do not wait until the Christmas season to buy Christmas presents. Purchase Christmas presents all year round. In fact, the biggest shopping day should be a few days after Christmas. Most items are reduced 70 percent. So make a list of things that you need and proactively look for them that day so you can take advantage of the savings. This is different from buying something on sale just because it is on sale. In this case you are doing so with a plan.

35. Buy clothes off season. If you buy swimsuits at the end of the summer, they are usually half price. Or buy your winter coat after the snow season has stopped. There's no longer a demand, and you can get a huge discount.

36. Do not buy designer clothes for babies! This boosts your self-esteem, not the baby's. A two-year-old is not aware of the latest fashion trends—and unless they can dunk, they don't need hundred-dollar sneakers.

37. If you purchase an item and it does not suit its purpose or you really do not like it when you get it home, do not put it in the back of your closet never to see it again. Take the time to return it and get your money back.

38. We already know the effects smoking has on the body. However, from a financial standpoint, consider the cost to keep up such a habit. With the cost of cigarette packs, the costs incurred to clean your clothes, your dental bills, and so on, the average cost is approximately $2,500 each year.

39. Forget the fact that alcohol is expensive; it is not conducive to you becoming wealthy. Nobody I know has told me they're successful because they drink.

40. Monitor your banking fees. They increase quickly.

41. Use your debt job to the fullest. You will get better value for your time and money. An added bonus, work at a store where you frequently shop. You can take advantage of the employee discount.

▶ *Mind-Set*

42. A credit card is not a solution to your problems; it is just a Band-Aid.

43. Do not take advice from people more messed up financially than you are.

44. Take care of what you already have.

45. Forget about keeping up with the Joneses. Keep up with your personal budget.

46. If your adult children live at home, they should be paying rent. Parents convince themselves that they are helping, but in reality they are handicapping their children. They are creating a false sense of reality. If your adult children pay rent that is comparable to what they would be charged by a stranger, you can save half and give it as a gift when they are ready to move out. If you do not, they will never move out!

47. Avoid buying things on sale just because they're on sale. There's nothing wrong with getting great deals when you have planned ahead. However, some people have closets or pantries full of stuff they do not use. But they always say, "It was 50 percent off, and I couldn't pass it up." Well, save 100 percent and don't buy it!

48. Avoid impulse buying! If you want to purchase gifts right before a holiday, the tendency is to spend more and bargain—shop less because of the time constraint. Budget your money during the year, and spend only what you have budgeted.

Intermediate Strategies

▶ *Low-Hanging Fruit*

49. Avoid heavy stock trading. The fees for commissions and taxes cut into the gains.

50. Do not hold on to stocks for sentimental reasons. If it is a bad company, you can cut that dog loose.

51. Invest in a 401(k) retirement plan or a traditional IRA. Pretax dollars are used for these plans. This is money you

will not have to pay to your least favorite relative, Uncle Sam—until you are taking the money out. Plus it grows tax free.

52. Avoid time-share programs. There are no real savings in this program. It is a monthly cost for an implied yearly vacation that you may never take. Then you're stuck with the burden of trying to find relatives or friends to use your time-share so that you can justify the cost.

53. If you have a bit of discretionary cash and would like to turn the cable back on, consider paying for only basic cable instead of all the premium channels. You will be surprised how little you miss them.

54. Buying in bulk is an excellent idea only if you have a large family. Bulk purchases usually go to waste if you don't consume them fast enough, therefore losing the money you originally intended to save.

55. Watch for sales on the grocery items you purchase on a regular basis. For example, I consume a large amount of frozen orange juice and lemonade. When those items are on sale, I buy as many as my freezer will hold. They usually last me until the next time they are on sale.

56. Instead of going out to the movies, rent a movie online and stream it to your TV, and make homemade popcorn. This can be a wonderful and economical family night.

57. Do not buy credit-card insurance, a form of insurance that will pay off your credit card if something happens to you. This insurance is billed to your card monthly and adds to your debt.

58. Do not always treat someone to dinner. Birthdays, business deals, anniversaries—celebrate these occasions over lunch. Lunch entrees are usually five to ten dollars less than dinner meals.

59. If you are already making IRA contributions, consider a tax-deferred annuity. These are new annuities without surrender charges. This type of annuity relieves you from incurring costs for taxes or capital gains and dividends until you reach age fifty-nine and a half.

▶ *Extra Effort*

60. Do not withdraw your pension, 401(k), or other retirement funds when you leave a job. You lose nearly half of it paying taxes and penalties. Contact an investment professional who can assist you in rolling a plan over to a professionally managed IRA so your money can continue to grow.

61. Avoid using more than two financial institutions. I know a man who had four IRA accounts at four banks and two different brokerage firms. Instead of paying a custodian at each financial institution, he could have placed them all in one location and saved hundreds of dollars yearly. Consolidation also makes it easier to review your progress, because you have only one financial statement instead of several.

62. When you travel, contact more than one travel agent, airline, or hotel chain. Ask about discount rates, off-season discounts, and travel packages.

63. Buy beverages and snacks in bulk. Stop worshipping vending machines. Those few dollars accumulate very quickly.

64. Avoid buying extravagant gifts for loved ones, friends, or even yourself that have no intrinsic value. Buy things that have a use or purpose, such as this book. (Hint, hint.)

65. Do not buy storage space! Have a ninety-day dump day: if you have not used it in ninety days, dump it.

66. Save your receipts on major purchases. If an item is broken, lost, or stolen, the credit-card company or merchandise warranty may apply. Also, if applicable, an insurance company will require confirmation of the cost to pay on a claim.

67. If you must treat someone to dinner, go to a restaurant featuring dinner specials. Take your dinner guests to a happy hour or free taco bar. This may raise a few eyebrows, but they are not paying your bills. I used to take coworkers out for their birthday and pretend to be pleasantly surprised at our luck when there was a special!

68. Encourage your college student to buy used textbooks.

69. Encourage your college student to participate in work-study programs. Working part-time while going to school never hurt anyone.

70. Make sure to keep records of all business and entertainment expenditures. Many people do not take tax credits for mileage, business meals, software purchases, and so on. I suggest consulting a professional tax advisor on this one.

71. When possible, refinance your home, and then use the surplus money to pay down debt. Then pay off your house. Think big! Do not just pay off installment debt; pay off ALL debt.

72. In cold climates, insulate your home and wrap the water heater. Pay this expense up front, and it will save you thousands of dollars in heating bills. Do not say you can't afford to insulate your home, unless you feel that you have the money to heat the outdoors surrounding your home.

73. Get several bids for major projects such as roofing, repairing a driveway, and installing a patio. Don't just go with the first person you speak with.

74. Pay half of your mortgage payment biweekly rather than the entire payment monthly. Biweekly payments equal twenty-six payments a year rather than the standard twelve. This amounts to thirteen full mortgage payments each year and could take thousands off your mortgage, and you will certainly have your home paid off at a faster rate. You do not have to carry a mortgage for the rest of your life. You could own it!

75. There's no law that requires you to carry a monthly car payment. Plan your future car purchase. How do you buy a new car? CASH!

76. When leasing a car, find out what the monthly payment would have been if you purchased and figure out the monthly difference. Then take that monthly difference and put it toward a mutual fund.

77. Avoid putting a higher-octane fuel in your vehicle. For example, using 87 rather than 92 premium does not make much difference.

78. Rather than spending money on costly car-insurance premiums, spend extra time searching out the most economical insurance rate.

79. When purchasing a new car, buy a car at the end of the year or, at the very least, at the end of the month. The sales staff will give you a better deal so they can make their monthly quota.

80. When you go to purchase a car, bring a calculator. Even if you do not know how to use it, just the sight of you calculating and figuring adds to your negotiating power.

81. Avoid paying full price for designer clothes! You can shop at outlet stores, purchase your clothes during the off-season, or shop during end-of-season sales.

82. Make your garments and shoes last. Take care of your clothes by keeping them clean and properly tailored. Put rubber soles and taps on the bottom of your shoes. This will add to their longevity.

▶ *Mind-Set*

83. Never invest in something you know nothing about.

84. Never purchase property you have not seen.

85. Do not allow your children to determine your grocery list. Many times children ask for items that catch their eye on TV, but they later end up not consuming them. Advertisers appeal to the sense of sight, not always the quality or sense of taste.

86. Do not buy anything simply because it's new and improved! If your current version works, why incur costs for minimal changes?

87. Avoid lending money to friends or relatives. Nine times out of ten, they will lose the money and/or damage the relationship. If you must lend money to family, secure collateral to ensure a return.

88. Be loyal to your service providers. Get to know them. For example, a good dry cleaner will sometimes negotiate rates if you use them often enough. They will also replace buttons and fix tears for free.

89. Set up a budget for your children while they're young. You are not their ATM machine.

90. Keep your money invested. Too much money is kept in low-interest savings accounts.

91. If you purchase a new car, pay off the car loan and keep the car for several years. The money you previously used

to pay your car note can now be used to invest in building wealth. Forget about keeping up with the Joneses; they are not wealthy.

92. Do not buy life insurance for children! When a child dies, the principal loss is emotional. Insurance is to indemnify and reimburse you for financial loss. Children do not contribute substantial income to the household. Therefore, the monthly premiums and life insurance for children could be better used elsewhere. The exception to this is making sure that you can cover any burial cost if your child does die prematurely.

Advanced Strategies

93. Make a charitable donation to a faith-based institution or charity. If you give stuff to a nonprofit, your tax deduction is based on its current market value rather than what you paid for it. You don't have to pay capital gains.

94. If you plan to start a business, write out a business plan. Do research on the venture, and do not enter any venture blindly!

95. Give stock as a gift on Christmas and birthdays—especially to children. This gift will grow with them.

Take Action:

Work Your "Saving like a Pro" To-Do List

Go through the "Saving like a Pro" section and pick three things that you can do this week to start saving better. Put a plan in place in your calendar and to-do list to make sure that you do the three things.

When you have completed those three things, go back to the list and look for three more that you can do. Continue this practice for as long as it takes you to work your way through the items that are relevant to you.

Introduction to Investing

What is your image of an investor? Do you have an image of somebody on Wall Street wearing an expensive suit and barking orders at other people to buy and sell stocks? Does it look like somebody that you don't see when you look in the mirror? If so, I'm going to let you in on a little secret today. Investors come in all shapes and sizes; you don't have to look a certain way or dress a certain way to take advantage of the power of investing. You just have to have some money, a plan, and some discipline.

But first, you need to understand the basics of investing so that you can stop being intimidated by the word "investing."

What Are Stocks, Bonds, and Mutual Funds?

If you already know what these terms mean, you can skim through this section, but I want to make sure that we are all on the same page with a few terms that are important to understand as an investor.

Publicly Listed Company

There are two kinds of companies, privately owned and publicly owned. A privately owned company becomes a publicly listed company in order to raise money. This is usually done so that the company can grow faster and bigger. They can raise money in one of two ways:

1. Issuing bonds
2. Issuing stocks

Bonds

When you buy a company's bond, you are making a loan to the company, which is raising money through obtaining debt. Bonds are like a loan that is distributed across a lot of debtors in the market. The company takes your money (principal) and in return pays you interest at predetermined intervals until you cash in the bond and get your principal back. The growth you can expect from bonds is conservative, and you do not have an ownership stake in the company.

Stocks

When you buy a company's stock, you are becoming a part owner of the company, so you get to benefit from the growth in the value of that company over time. Unlike with bonds, for which there is a predetermined amount that you will make over time with your ownership, you can experience a much wider range of wealth creation with stocks because you have ownership. A company's earnings drive its stock price, so you get to benefit from the good times of the company, but you also take a hit if the company's value drops.

There are two ways you can make money from owning stock. The first is by the growth in how much your shares are worth. For example, if you buy a stock for ten dollars and two years later it is worth a hundred dollars, your share increased in value by ninety dollars, and so if you sell it, that is what you earned by owning it.

The second way you can make money from stock ownership is from dividends. This is money the company pays from its earnings to all its shareholders based on how many shares they hold. Not all companies pay dividends; those that do are usually referred to as income or dividend-paying stocks. When you hear the term "blue-chip stock," it usually refers to the stock of an established company that pays dividends.

Capital Gains

This is another term for the money you earn from an investment. When a stock goes up in value, the amount that your value in shares goes up is called capital gains. This money is considered taxable income at the end of the year if you sell the stock and cash in on the income.

Mutual Funds

Mutual funds are a great way to get started with investing because they are a way for you to pool your money with other investors and get a more diversified exposure to the market. Buying a mutual fund is like riding a bus; you get onto the bus and pay a fare, and then somebody else does the driving to get you to your destination, which is determined by the overall goal of the mutual fund. So you find a mutual fund whose goal aligns with your investment goal, and a professional investment manager makes the decisions about how to distribute the investment within the mutual fund to align to the goal.

Too few people take advantage of this strategy because of their lack of knowledge. But there are several benefits to investing in mutual funds, and I recommend them as a good starting place as a beginning investor. As I mentioned before, in a mutual fund, you and other investors pool your money to purchase securities. This tactic gives you the opportunity to share ownership in several different companies. Let's explore mutual fund benefits further.

Professional management. You have a professional manager who is well versed in investing. Few people have the knowledge or time to study and analyze stocks, economic conditions, and trends; therefore it is wise to hire a person or a team to manage your money. A mutual fund manager makes buy and sell decisions and has the benefit of getting advice from many analysts and strategists. In other words, you don't have to be an expert to invest; you just have to know one.

Diversification. An advantage you have with a mutual fund is that when you invest, you are diversified over many companies. A mutual fund may have as many as a hundred companies. You can own dozens of securities that would normally be too expensive to purchase individually. You can invest in many sectors with one mutual fund. This is beneficial because if you own one security, when it goes down, you go down, but if you own several companies, when one of those companies goes down by itself, it has a minor impact on your entire portfolio.

Convenience. If you own a mutual fund, you are given a statement and periodic paperwork on the status of the fund from the firm holding your mutual fund. When tax time rolls around, you are sent a statement containing all capital gains and dividends information. You can reinvest profits back into the fund for free. You can invest in the fund monthly. Also, most mutual funds belong to a family of funds. As your objectives change, you can switch to a different fund within the family and not incur a sales charge. Mutual funds can also be put in brokerage accounts, IRAs, Roth IRAs, 401(k)s, 403(b)s, and other retirement plans.

Regulation. The Investment Company Act of 1940 contains a myriad of rules that mutual funds (investment companies) have to abide by. There are also several other federal and state laws that mutual funds must adhere to. The Securities and Exchange Commission (SEC) oversees them. This regulation is designed to protect investors by requiring mutual funds to clearly define the risks of investing, report performance consistently, operate within prescribed standards, and observe antifraud rules in the buying and selling of fund shares.

Liquidity. If you want your money back from a mutual fund, it is easy to get it. You just put in a request to sell your shares, and within seven days of the sale, you get your money. So unlike real estate or your bicycle, where you have to go and find a buyer in order to get cash, a mutual fund is easy to liquidate if you need access to the funds.

Discipline. One of my favorite attributes of mutual funds is that they encourage discipline by eliminating the need for you to make buy or sell decisions. The investment manager does that for you, and your sole responsibility is to make sure you consistently add more money to your investment. Most first-time investors do not have the intestinal fortitude to buy or hold on to securities when the market is down. But with a mutual fund, you have a manager doing that for you, so it takes away the anxiety of navigating those situations, ensuring that you keep your money invested for the long haul, which is how your wealth will successfully grow.

Affordable. Mutual funds have low initial cost. You can start with as little as $250 or a low monthly investment of $50 a month. With those funds, you get a diversified, regulated, convenient, liquid, and professionally managed portfolio. This is probably one of the best ways for investors to leverage their time and knowledge when starting out.

There are several different types of mutual funds, and there are more mutual funds than stocks on the New York Stock Exchange. The best fund for you is determined by your risk tolerance and your time horizon. Like anything else, the higher the risk, the higher the return.

If you have to pay for your child's education within the next three months, then putting your money in the stock market would not be a good idea. That would be like taking a plane to travel three blocks. If you are saving for your retirement ten years away, keeping your money in the money market would not be a wise utilization of your money. That would be like walking from Los Angeles to New York and back again. You must choose the right investment to make your investment life easier, efficient, and more profitable.

Develop Your New Eyes

In addition to starting your investment activity by buying a mutual fund and taking advantage of all its benefits, it is important for you to develop what I call new eyes in the way you look at investments in the market and spot good opportunities. Remember, earnings drive stock prices, and earnings are driven by how well a company is doing. So if you want to become good at picking stocks to invest your money in, you need to become good at identifying well-run companies that are going to have strong earnings that continue to grow. It is not enough just to look at the stock prices.

There are three attributes I look for when I determine whether to pursue a particular stock: great products and services, great management, and intrinsic value. You can use an exercise I teach my students to begin developing your own new eyes to find these attributes.

The best way to start is to walk through your day mentally and think about each of the products and services that you have used since you woke up. Think about when your alarm went off and which company made that electronic device or smartphone.

Then think about which department store you bought the sheets on your bed from. Think about the company that made the toothpaste you brushed your teeth with after you got out of bed, and the soap you used for your shower. Think about the pharmaceutical company that made the medication you took in the morning and the pharmacy you bought that medication from. Think about the company that made the food you ate for breakfast and the car company that made the car you got into for your commute. Before you even get to work, you have interacted with over a dozen companies that are most likely good starting points for you to examine as possible investments.

As you go through the exercise, jot down ten to fifteen company names, and then start doing research on them. Consider their full line of products and services, and note whether they are especially innovative or dominant in their markets. What about the management of the company? How well run are they?

Then, is there some intrinsic value of the company's product or service? Intrinsic value is one of my favorite indicators of whether a company is a good candidate to buy. Intrinsic value is when a company sells something at a premium that people are willing to pay. The higher the premium, the better. For example, when sneakers cost less than $10 a pair to make but sell for $100 or even $200 plus per pair, then the difference between $10 and the sale price is the intrinsic value.

To illustrate this concept even further, let me tell you about my relatives who came from out of state to visit me in Los Angeles. We decided to go to a national amusement park, and when we got there, we had to pay thirty dollars per person just to gain entry. Once inside with my new-eyes vision, I noticed many of the other tourists buying seventy-dollar sweatshirts and tank tops. My new eyes also allowed me to see that tourists were buying three-dollar soft drinks to chase their six-dollar hamburgers. I asked myself,

"Could I invite people over to my house and charge thirty dollars to come in, serve hot dogs and soda for ten dollars, and put my face on a sweatshirt and sell it for seventy dollars?" Clearly I couldn't, so I decided the only way I could buy into this scenario was to buy stock in the company, which is what I did.

As you use your new eyes more frequently, you will begin to spot opportunities like this everywhere, and as you get better at doing so, you will become a better decision maker in terms of which stocks might be a good fit for your goals.

Five Keys to Retiring Comfortably

Not everybody has to think about funding college education, but everybody needs to think about how to pay for retirement. This is especially important because unlike with college education, you cannot borrow money for your retirement. So it is important to have an investment plan for your retirement as early as possible in your earning career.

There are five keys to retiring comfortably:

▶ *Key #1: Start Right Now*

The most important thing to do when it comes to retirement investments, regardless of how close you are to retirement, is to start. If you don't take action, you will not get an outcome. So make a commitment, if you haven't already, to ensure that you have an investment plan in place for your retirement, and then get it started.

▶ *Key #2: Utilize Tools from the Government*

Make sure to take advantage of whichever government-qualified plan you are eligible to use. If you work at a for-profit company, you should take advantage of the 401(k) if your company provides it, especially if it provides matching funds because that is free money. If you work at a nonprofit, there may be a 403(b), and if you are self-employed, you can take advantage of an SEP program. If your employer does not provide a 401(k) or 403(b), you can open up an IRA.

These tools are important to use because they provide you with a tax deduction (thus lowering your taxes for the current year), and the investments in them can grow tax deferred, which means you get the benefit of greater gains than if your money were being taxed for capital gains in the year you earned it.

▶ Key #3: Make It Automatic

Your retirement savings is not something that you want to leave up to your monthly financial whims. You want to set up your plan; set up consistent, automatic payments; and then leave it alone. The best way to do this is to have contributions automatically deducted from your paycheck. If you have a 401(k) or 403(b) at work, this is usually provided as an option from your employer. If you have an IRA or a SEP, set up an automatic withdrawal from your bank account monthly so that the money comes out without any action needed from you.

▶ Key #4: Start Collecting Eggs

Think of your retirement investing as a process of collecting eggs and putting them into baskets. You don't want to eat the eggs before they hatch; instead, you want to give them an opportunity to grow and hatch into full chickens which will in turn be able to lay more eggs and multiply your collection. So focus on collection only until it is time for you to retire; this is not money that you should see as available for other uses.

► *Key #5: Learn to Diversify*

As your investments accumulate over time for your retirement, make sure that you are not putting all your eggs in one basket. This is important to protect you from changes in the market. You want to develop a portfolio that counterbalances itself; when one part of it is down, another part goes up, so overall your portfolio grows, and you have secure funds for when you retire.

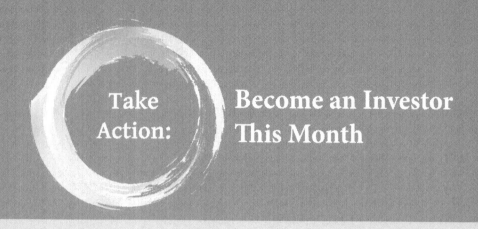

I f you currently buy lunch or coffee every day, you probably spend about $9 per day. For the next month, find a way to substitute those expenses so that you are saving about $63 per week, or about $250 per month. Instead of spending that money on anything else consumable, open up a mutual fund with an investment professional and commit to putting in that $250 every month. To ensure your success with this, have the money taken out of your paycheck directly and put into the mutual fund every time you get paid.

Congratulations, you just became an investor. Now wasn't that easy?

Chapter 8:

Building Your Wealth Machine

WHOEVER CAN BE TRUSTED WITH VERY LITTLE CAN ALSO
BE TRUSTED WITH MUCH, AND WHOEVER IS DISHONEST
WITH VERY LITTLE WILL ALSO BE DISHONEST WITH MUCH.

—Luke 6:10

At the beginning of this book, I spoke about the misconception that wealthy people engage in wrongdoing and selfishness. There is an underlying sentiment that the wealthy build their wealth by taking advantage of those who have less, when the opposite should actually be true if you are going to build legacy wealth that is long lasting—especially if you are a Christian.

One of the most critical qualities for building wealth the right way is character—who you are when nobody is watching and there is no chance of getting caught. This is the true reflection of the kind of impact God has in your life, and spills over into the way you deal with finances. If you are comfortable operating in gray

Chapter 8: Building Your Wealth Machine

areas, instead of taking the straight path to get to your goals, you may be successful for a season, but eventually your actions will catch up to you.

The reason I am spending some time on this area is that when you are in the struggling and steady stages, you are doing the best to survive, and there is a certain humility that comes with that situation because you know that you need help. When you begin moving into solid, surplus, and service, it is easy to start believing that your success is solely because of you—and this is where your level of character will catch up to you. If you have built a character of honesty and productivity as you worked through the earlier stages, when it comes to building your wealth machine, you will naturally gravitate toward methods that are squeaky clean, because it is more important for you to preserve your character than to build wealth quickly.

However, if you haven't worked on your character, the last three stages can be dangerous because as you build more wealth, you experience more freedom in how you spend both your money and your time. The impacts of your decisions become greater as your resources increase; there are more people that can be helped or hurt by you, and therefore your responsibility in stewardship is even greater.

This chapter, "Building Your Wealth Machine," focuses on strategies for three key areas you should include in your portfolio to work on the Increase and Distribute sections of the Wealth Cycle: real estate, investments, and business. I am going to teach you a mixture of mind-set and techniques that will help you take advantage of the wealth-building power of each of these areas. These are not get-rich-quick approaches and therefore require strategy, planning, and patience. They also require partnership with others to build a team around you that can support you in your wealth-building goals, because the biggest waste of your time is to try to be an expert at everything. Learn enough to make intelligent decisions and to pick the experts that can advise you on the details. This will free you up to focus on constantly looking out for opportunities, instead of getting tied up running things. This does not mean that you are not intimately involved in your financial affairs; it just means that as you build wealth, the sheer volume of what you need to oversee grows, and you don't have the capacity to be involved in every last detail of your portfolio.

Building Your Wealth Team

PLANS FAIL FOR LACK OF COUNSEL,
BUT WITH MANY ADVISERS THEY SUCCEED.
—Proverbs 15:22

Before you begin the process of accelerating your Increase and Distribute activities, the first part of building your wealth machine is identifying the right team to surround yourself with. If you follow any team sports, you probably understand this concept quite well. Regardless of how great a player is, he or she cannot play all of the positions on the court or the field. In order for a player's greatness to shine, he or she is dependent on a team that will at least keep the player in the game.

If you want to win in your finances, your team should consist of all-star players in each of the following roles:

1. Financial advisor
2. Accountant
3. Estate lawyer (plus real estate and business lawyers if needed)

Your Financial Advisor

Your financial advisor is like the quarterback or point guard of your financial team. When this person is really good, he or she sees the full picture and guides you in ways to use the rest of your team to maximize your success. If you are serious about building wealth, the person who plays this role should not be winging it. Just as you would not want somebody who watches a lot of episodes of *ER* or *Grey's Anatomy* but has no medical training to operate on you, you do not want an amateur financial hobbyist to be the source of your financial-planning direction.

Sound financial advice should come from a professional because a good relationship with a qualified investment professional can only enhance your results. Financial professionals are called several different names, such as financial advisor, financial planner, financial consultant, and stockbroker. It's not what they're called so much as what they do. For the sake of simplicity, I will use the term "financial advisor" going forward.

The challenge is to locate the right financial advisor. The best way to find one is through a referral. Ask friends, family, or a neighborhood leader that you respect, such as your pastor. Once you receive a referral, meet and talk to the prospective advisor. Here are some questions you may want to ask:

1. Who are your typical clients? The typical client should have a profile similar to yours.
2. Who do you specialize in, or what are your areas of expertise? The advisor's area of expertise should coincide with your desired goals.
3. What type of investments do you use? The advisor's explanations should be clear and concise. If he or she does not take the time to explain investments to you clearly, time will show that he or she does not have the patience you require.

4. How are you compensated? The advisor's compensation model should fit the type of relationship you want to have with him or her. Financial advisors are compensated in one of three ways:

   a. *Commission*—when a security is bought or sold, a commission is charged

   b. *Fee only*—a flat annual or hourly fee

   c. *Fee based*—compensation on a percentage of the money under management

It's important to understand the underlying motivation for each of the compensation models so you can evaluate the advice you are receiving.

When advisors work on commission, they are paid to buy and sell stock. They make money from buying and selling, not from investment performance—so even if the investments don't perform, as long as they are doing transactions, they are making money.

The challenge with a fee-only arrangement is that an hourly charge often discourages clients from seeking advice when they should. Determine whether this will be the case for you.

With a fee-based compensation model, you and the advisor are on the same side of the table. The only way for the advisor to make more money is to grow your assets. The advisor has to work smarter for the money.

Once you pick your financial advisor, make sure to meet with him or her!

The most important role the financial advisor plays in the beginning is to understand your goals and help you develop a plan to achieve them. Most financial goals fall into one of these areas: savings, retirement, college planning, or building wealth. Aspects of financial planning include these:

- Cash management and budgeting
- Insurance
- Investment management

- Retirement planning
- Estate planning

Once your advisor has established a plan with you, he or she helps you to monitor the plan and make adjustments as your life evolves, because things always change—and you want to make sure that your financial plans change along with them.

Your Accountant

> IN THIS WORLD NOTHING CAN BE SAID TO BE CERTAIN,
> EXCEPT DEATH AND TAXES.
>
> —Benjamin Franklin

Taxes will always be one of your biggest expenses, but there are ways to ensure that you don't overpay on taxes, if you have a tax management plan in place. This is one of the most important reasons to have an accountant on your team; an accountant can help you foresee things that impact you from a tax perspective and make sure you make the right decisions that are in your favor.

There is nothing wrong with minimizing taxes by paying only what you owe. It is when you try to evade taxes that you should legitimately be paying that you are doing something illegal. When evaluating the accountant for your team, make sure that it is somebody who operates with character and does not even recommend any strategies that would put you in a gray area with the Internal Revenue Service.

In addition to helping you with taxes, an accountant is critical in helping you create ways to measure all the aspects of your wealth portfolio. When you are dealing with businesses and real estate, an accountant is especially helpful in helping you think about what metrics you need to monitor to ensure that your investments are performing the way you expect.

Your Lawyers

Law is a vast area of knowledge, and when you are looking for legal representation as a part of your team, you need to ensure that you focus on getting specialists in the areas that you need. Rather than getting a generalist lawyer that handles all of your legal needs because you think this will save you money, make sure to get specialized lawyers for these three areas that are critical to building your wealth machine: estate, business, and real estate law.

Estate Lawyer

If you are truly building a financial legacy, you have to have a plan in place for when you eventually die. This is an inevitability that none of us are exempt from—unless you are still living when Jesus comes. So planning for what should happen with your hard-earned wealth when you die should be a high priority—especially if you have a spouse and/or children. This includes your will, your power of attorney, your trusts, and a whole host of specialized vehicles that you need depending on your situation and assets.

In addition to your financial advisor's input into your estate planning, it is important to have a good lawyer on your team that specializes in estate law, because there are a lot of legal structures that need to be in place for your plan to be solid. This is especially important as your net worth increases and you have more assets in your portfolio.

Business Lawyer

If you are starting or taking over a business, make sure to get the services of a lawyer that specializes in business law. A business lawyer can correctly advise you on how to set up your business legally based on what you plan to do, and will help you set up other legal structures as the business grows to ensure that you have the right level of legal protection to preserve the wealth and value in the business. People love to sue businesses, so you have to be set up correctly to ensure that you are protected from that liability in all the different ways it can come.

Real Estate Lawyer

When you start expanding your wealth portfolio into real estate, you realize many legal interactions are required to be successful. Real estate law is very specific to geography, so it is important that you find somebody who specializes not only in real estate law but also in the locations where you are purchasing and managing properties. Real estate law can vary widely by state; make sure that the person you are dealing with knows all the intricacies for the state where you are investing. If you are investing in multiple states, you may need to have more than one real estate lawyer—one for each state where you invest—to ensure that you have the right coverage.

Your Real Estate Agent

If you are serious about investing in real estate, an indispensable member of your team will be your real estate agent. Unless you are a real estate agent yourself, you need the help of a professional to find the right properties for your goals and then to negotiate and secure the right deals to acquire them. As much as you may think you understand how to find properties yourself, you will always be at a disadvantage to somebody whose full-time job is to understand a local real estate market and know what deals are available.

As with the legal side of real estate, you will probably have to deal with a handful of real estate agents if you invest in widely varying geographies, because the value a real estate agent brings to you is knowledge of a local market. There are things real estate agents will know about the properties on the market that you just can't find out by looking on the Internet, and it is this knowledge that makes your real estate agent a valuable member of your team.

Your Contractor/Handyman/Inspector

When you move beyond your primary residence and start purchasing investment properties, it is important to assemble your own team of contractors, handymen, and inspectors that can assist you with the renovation and maintenance of your investments. When you are purchasing a property that needs renovation, these team members are especially valuable because they can help you accurately assess how much money you will need to put into a property before you can rent it out or sell it. The accuracy of these types of estimates can make the difference between a very good deal and one where you lose a lot of money, so make sure you build up a team of specialists in these contracting trades.

Investment Strategy

SUPPOSE ONE OF YOU WANTS TO BUILD A TOWER. WON'T YOU FIRST SIT DOWN AND ESTIMATE THE COST TO SEE IF YOU HAVE ENOUGH MONEY TO COMPLETE IT? FOR IF YOU LAY THE FOUNDATION AND ARE NOT ABLE TO FINISH IT, EVERYONE WHO SEES IT WILL RIDICULE YOU, SAYING, "THIS PERSON BEGAN TO BUILD AND WASN'T ABLE TO FINISH."

—Luke 14:28–30

In the previous chapter, I gave you some foundational information and strategies to get your life as an investor going. Once you have mastered those techniques and generated more surplus income, you can begin to develop a more sophisticated investment strategy. Since I am not your financial advisor, I will not make any specific recommendations, but I can give you a framework that you can use to guide your decision making in your investment strategy.

The framework consists of three concepts:
1. Diversify your portfolio.
2. Manage your buckets.
3. Manage your risk.

Diversify Your Portfolio

As you develop more financial resources and have more options for where to put your money, it is important to have a simple framework through which you can evaluate your entire portfolio. One of the key principles that you should always maintain with your investments is to ensure that you are appropriately diversified for your current financial goals.

This chart shows you how I generally explain the different layers that your investment portfolio should contain:

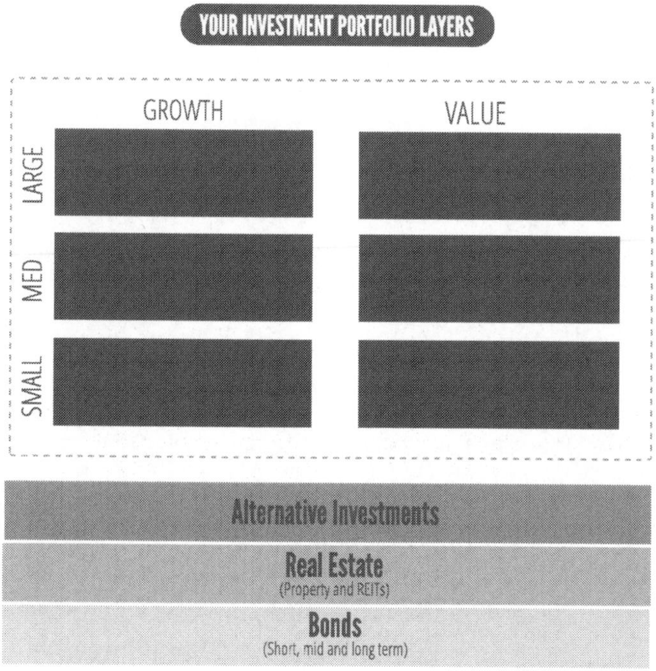

Figure 6: Your Investment Portfolio "Layers"

The layers are bonds, real estate, alternative investments, and small, medium, and large companies with categories for growth and value.

Let's look at bonds first. There are three types of bonds: short-term, medium-term, and long-term bonds. The type depends on how long you hold them; typically the longer that you hold the bond, the higher the interest rate. And the shorter the time you hold it, the lower the interest rate. Within bonds, there are three categories: municipal bonds, US savings bonds, and corporate bonds. Municipal bonds are free from state and city tax, while US savings bonds are free from federal taxes. Corporate bonds typically pay higher interest than municipal or government bonds because they involve more risk, and their interest is taxable.

The next layer in your diversified portfolio is real estate. The first way to get into real estate is to own your own residence and/or your own properties. If a property has fewer than five units, it's called residential. If there are more than five units, it's called commercial real estate. There is also another area of real estate. There's a security called a real estate investment trust (REIT). Through this type of investment, you can have ownership in shopping centers, malls, and properties like these that are owned jointly between you and other investors (similar to mutual funds) and are managed by professional investment managers on your behalf. You can also own international REITs.

The next layer is alternative investments. These investments include things such as gold, silver, hard assets, and even real estate. The defining criterion of an alternative investment is that it doesn't fluctuate as much as other securities with the US market or it has an opposite effect as those securities. If the markets go down, alternative investments will go up, so you always want to have room in your portfolio for them.

The next layer is the bread and butter of your portfolio: small, medium, and large companies that you own through purchasing stock. Small means emerging companies who come up with an idea for a product or service and have started growing their idea into a business. All companies start small before they go to medium and then to large. A medium company is not yet ubiquitous in your daily life, but it's in most places nationally, and a large company is one you can't go through the day without utilizing. These investments can be divided in two categories. The first is value. Value means the stocks trade cheaply. Large value means it's a dividend-paying company, a company that's pretty steady with long records of increased earnings and dividends. The second category is growth stocks, which can grow at 20 percent per year or have a pattern of growth and are consistently expanding. You don't want to have all your eggs, all your money, in one area. What you want to do is diversify those assets.

Manage Your Buckets

In addition to diversifying your portfolio, it is important to manage the buckets that catch your income as it comes in. There are two ways to think about those buckets. The first kind of bucket has to do with the way you distribute your income across different risk horizons.

In the Risk Horizon figure below you will see that funds which are needed in the shorter term should be in more conservative investments that are easier to get to – more liquid. So the buckets to the left are where you would hold those investments. This is primarily your zero to twelve month and two to three-year horizon. As the time that you need the funds becomes longer, you can use riskier and less liquid investment vehicles because you can handle larger fluctuations in the value of the investment during a longer investment term. You are rewarded for keeping the money in the investments longer by the opportunity for larger returns.

Conservative/Liquid   More Risk/Illiquid

Figure 7: Risk Horizon Buckets

The second kind of bucket has to do with the asset-use categories that you catch your income in. There are three of these buckets. Some of your assets should go into a consumption bucket; these are assets that you need to live on and enjoy life. The second bucket is your contingency bucket, or your "just in case of an emergency" bucket. Third is the custodial bucket: assets that are not needed during your working lifetime but are intended for your retirement and to pass on after you die. These assets will outlive you and can be for family, friends, or charity. We tend to fill the buckets in that order—consumption, contingency, and then custodial—but it is important to make sure that you correctly manage the consumption bucket so that enough attention is given to the contingency and custodial buckets—especially the custodial bucket, because it is your legacy.

How much of your paycheck is going toward building your financial legacy?

Figure 8: The Three Asset Buckets

Manage Your Risk

Risk is inevitable when it comes to investing. There are only four things you can do with risk. The first is to ignore it. If you're driving a car, this means that you don't get car insurance. You drive whatever car you want (regardless of condition), do whatever you want, and ignore the fact that there's risk. The second is to avoid it. Don't get in the car. You want to go from point A to point B, but you just stay at home all the time. Third is to take a managed risk approach, which you should practice. In our example, you would manage your risk by driving according to the rules of the road and keeping your car well maintained. Put your hands at nine and three, and map out where you're going. The fourth approach is also highly recommended; this is to transfer risk. That means getting car insurance so that a third party will pay the cost for an accident, and it doesn't come out of your assets. These are the four ways you can manage risk, so my question to you is, "How are you managing your risk when it comes to your investments or other areas of your financial life?" You can't ignore or avoid it by not investing altogether, because then you are just staying where you are and not progressing. Instead, focus on managing and transferring risk. Transferring risk would also be getting life, long-term care, or disability insurance.

Figure 9: Dealing with Risk

Real Estate Strategy

THE HIGHEST HEAVENS BELONG TO THE LORD,
BUT THE EARTH HE HAS GIVEN TO MANKIND.

—Psalm 115:16

Real estate is a critical component of any serious wealth-building plan. There are three attributes that are especially attractive about this type of investment:

- *Intrinsic value.* No two properties are the same, and there is a finite amount of land available in any given geographical area. This means that you can get a premium on a piece of property by buying it before an area becomes popular and benefit from the increase in value when the area becomes more sought after.
- *Proactive value creation.* You can also proactively increase the value of your property by making improvements through renovations and landscaping.
- *Income generating.* Properties you purchase to rent out can not only increase in value over time but also provide you with steady income when your tenants pay you.

Along with the benefits of real estate are some risks and responsibilities that you should know about and plan for before you invest. Because each property is unique, there can be unknown issues with a piece of real estate that you discover only after you have made the investment. To mitigate this risk, it is important to have a strong team of professionals that do inspections and contracting work so that you can find as much as possible ahead of time and know how much it will cost to fix.

With real estate, you are also subject to the trends of a particular geographic area. If there is an event or a series of events that causes the properties around you to lose value, your property will lose value as well. You can mitigate this risk by always ensuring that you don't buy at the top of a market, especially if there is a real estate bubble in that area. It is always best to find the ugliest house on a pretty block and invest in fixing it up so that you don't overpay.

If you own properties with tenants, you need to have a game plan ahead of time for how you will handle both maintenance of the properties and troublesome tenants. You have to have strong legal representation and liability protection to ensure that your investment does not negatively impact the rest of your portfolio.

In terms of your strategy for investing in real estate, sticking with a simple plan that embodies these four principles will help you be very successful:

1. Make and keep your credit great.
2. Use patience and discipline.
3. Get cash-flow properties.
4. Use the debt multiplier

Make and Keep Your Credit Great

Your credit score has a direct impact on the interest rate you are charged to get a mortgage. And the interest rate on a mortgage determines how expensive it is for you to buy a piece of real estate. So an important part of your investment strategy for real estate should be to guard your credit score and keep it high. If you have a low credit score, it may even be worth it for you to wait until it has improved before you start buying real estate.

If you want to maintain a good credit score, do the following:

- Pay everything on time.
- Develop long relationships with creditors; don't cancel a credit card even if you have cut it up.
- Protect your credit; get a credit report every year to check balances, and do not cosign for others.
- Keep a low debt-to-credit ratio.

In addition, if you currently have a low credit score, here are five tips to help you build it up:

- Get your credit report. Dispute any inaccuracies with a certified letter, and ask the credit agencies to remove or delete them.
- Pay your bills on time.
- Keep open the credit lines you have had the longest; use only one personal and one business card.
- Manage your credit and do not open credit accounts you don't plan to use. Do not open a lot of accounts at once.
- Keep balances low; if you have a $10,000 credit limit, don't keep $9,990 charged on it.

Use Patience and Discipline

When you are buying real estate, time is your best friend. Never rush into the purchase of a property, because the worst deals happen when you are desperate. Give yourself time to get qualified for the right mortgage, identify the right property, and make the necessary improvements to the property (if necessary) before you start using it. This principle is true whether you are buying your first home or your fiftieth investment property.

There are three things that you will do each time you purchase a property: get qualified, identify a property, and buy smart. So it is important to know the right way to do each of them.

Get Qualified

For most people, getting qualified means that a financial institution determines how much money it is willing to lend you for a mortgage. Creditors do this by looking at four components of your financial situation:

- Your income
- Your assets
- Your employment
- Your credit

When they look at your income, they are trying to determine whether you have enough money coming in to make each of your monthly mortgage payments on time. They consider all your sources of income, so if you are married, they may look at both your and your spouse's income. If you have multiple sources of income other than your primary job, they consider those as well, provided you can show the reliability of that income on a monthly basis.

Creditors look at your assets in relation to your liabilities. Assets are things that have and can appreciate in value, and liabilities are what you owe other people. It is in your favor if your assets are greater than your liabilities, so focus on eliminating your debt before purchasing property. Examples of the kinds of assets creditors look at are your bank accounts and brokerage accounts that are liquid and could be sold to cover your debt.

Your employment is reviewed from two angles: where you work (including how much you make) and how long you have worked there. The longer the income history you can show, the less risky it is for the financial institution to lend you money, so a good job track record works in your favor. Even if you have switched jobs recently, it's okay if you stayed in the same field and continued in the same income range, because the pattern is consistent.

The final component, your credit, is probably the one that causes people the most anxiety. It is also the area that has the most significant impact on the interest rate of your mortgage. There is no need for this area to be scary if you understand what the financial institution is reviewing when it looks at your credit. Just remember that your credit score is impacted by the following things:

- Type of credit used
- Payment history
- Amounts owed
- Length of credit
- New credit

Of these areas, payment history and amounts owed have the highest weighting.

Once the creditors build up your profile based on your income, assets, employment, and credit information, they use the three Cs to determine whether to lend money to you and how much they are willing to lend. The three Cs stand for character, capital, and capacity.

Character is an examination of whether you intend to repay your debts. These are the kinds of questions the financial institution asks:

- Have you used credit before?
- Do you pay on time?
- Do you have a good credit report?
- How long have you lived at your address?

Capital looks at your resources for repaying the debt. Creditors look at these kinds of things:

- What property do you already own?
- How much money do you have in savings?
- Do you have investments that can be used as collateral?

Capacity examines whether you can repay the debt. These are the types of questions reviewed:

- Do you have a steady job?
- How long have you been at your present job?
- What is your salary?
- How many other loan payments do you have (are you over-dosing on debt)?
- What are your current living expenses?
- What are your debts and dependencies?

Once the lender determines that it is willing to lend you money, the biggest factor driving how much it lends you is your income. The lender wants to make sure that you can afford what you buy, so your qualification letter always includes a maximum amount that the lender will lend you. The biggest mistake I see people making is to look at the number on their qualification letter and use it as the starting point for the prices of houses that they start visiting. You are setting yourself up for disaster if you do this, because you leave no room for any contingency, and you will inevitably buy too much house for your financial situation.

Determine how the maximum amount the lender is willing to lend you translates into a monthly payment, and compare that to what you pay for housing today. For example, if you are currently paying $1,000 per month in rent and you qualify for a mortgage with payments of $2,500, you have to be sure you can keep up with that jump in your budget for housing expenses. A very good way to test this is to save the difference between what you pay now for housing and what you qualified for over a period of three to six months, and see whether you can keep up with it. In our example, you should see whether you can save $1,500 per month comfortably before you decide to take on that $2,500-per-month mortgage. On several occasions, I've had people do this exercise and come back to me saying, "I can't save $1,500 per month." Guess what: that means they can't afford that $2,500 mortgage!

Even if you can save the $1,500 per month, I still recommend that you look for property that is priced at about 70 percent of the mortgage that you are qualified for. For example, if you qualified for a $500,000 mortgage, look for property in the $350,000 range. This is especially important if you are a first-time homebuyer and are moving from renting to owning, because home ownership introduces a lot of costs that you currently don't have to think about as a renter, including maintenance and lawn care, to name just a couple.

A qualification also has a time limit before the lender has to requalify you, so it is important that you don't do things that can alter your credit score while you are looking to buy property. Don't start opening up additional credit cards or cosigning for people, because each inquiry on your credit report will affect your score. In terms of cosigning, as I have mentioned before, even if you are not buying real estate, this is never a good idea, because cosigning is like giving people a piggyback ride when they should be walking for themselves—and in the process, taking on the risk of their financial behavior.

Identify a Property

Once you are qualified for a mortgage, the next step to acquire a property is to go out and find one that fits your goals. Again, avoid looking at the top of your price range, but find something that you can comfortably afford.

There are three types of properties that you can purchase:

- *Turnkey.* This is a move-in-ready property that requires little to no work. When you buy this type of property, you will pay top dollar because there are no factors that bring the price down.
- *Light renovation.* These are properties that need a little bit of work before they are the way you want them. Sometimes

this may include fixing a few minor things and painting. It might include replacing some cabinetry or fixtures, but there is no major electrical, plumbing, or structural work required. You need to budget for the fixes required and include that in your evaluation of the investment.

- *Total makeovers.* These are properties that you have to completely redo. The renovation cost is usually in the tens and sometimes hundreds of thousands, so you have to make sure that you have the financial resources to cover the cost of the repairs, including some contingency funds. If you have the financial resources for this type of property, they tend to be the best deals because you can pick them up cheaply since they are harder to sell to people who are looking for turnkey or light-renovation properties. You can also get the home of your dreams because you can customize the makeover to your preferences.

Buy Smart

Just as you have to develop new eyes when investing in stocks, you need to develop new eyes for the way you determine what properties to buy. This should be the case even when you are purchasing your primary residence, because it is usually your first real estate investment.

If you look for a property the way most people approach the task, you probably list out all the things you want in your ideal house or investment property, and then pick a list of areas that you find attractive to purchase in. If you have children, the location is most likely heavily influenced by the quality of the schools in that particular municipality. You then provide this list of wants to your real estate agent, who starts giving you options to check out until you find a house that fits.

There is nothing wrong with this approach, especially for your primary residence, but if you want to develop your new eyes as a real estate investor, you have to ask yourself a different set of questions in addition to the primary ones above. Expand your search to locations that are not yet the hot place to buy but are likely to develop in a few years. You can determine which areas have this profile by looking at the trends surrounding the area. Are there plans for a new shopping area or stadium near that area? Is there a mix of newly built homes and homes that need fixing up? Is it an area that had a lot of foreclosures but still has a good school system and is accessible for commuters? What other major plans to develop the area are being discussed by the local government?

When you start asking yourself these kinds of questions, you begin to look at your real estate portfolio in a whole new light, and opportunities that others have not yet capitalized on become accessible to you. The more you can find these types of opportunities, the better your chances of buying undervalued property that will appreciate in the future and increase the value of your real estate portfolio.

Get Cash-Flow Properties

When looking for a property to purchase, look for one that already has its profit built in. Buying a property because you believe it will go up in value and that is the only way you expect to make money is called speculation and can get you into a lot of trouble if you overpay for the property and its value goes down. I am particularly fond of multifamily residential units that have a positive cash flow from day one when I purchase them. Even if the property never goes up in value, I know that I will make money with it because it is income generating. If you are looking for your first home, buying a two- or three-family instead of a single-family home is an excellent choice because your tenants' rent will offset the cost of your mortgage, and you will be able to pay off the mortgage faster.

Use the Debt Multiplier

Just because mortgages are good debt doesn't mean that you should hold them for a long time if you can help it. You used the Debt Eliminator to get out of consumer debt; use the same technique to pay off the mortgage, first on your primary residence and then on your investment properties. This is an especially powerful strategy for rental properties because over time the net cash flow of the properties increases dramatically when you eliminate the mortgage, which is your largest expense on the property. If you own multiple properties, organize their mortgage payments in the same way you did your credit cards in the debt-multiplier section; attack one mortgage at a time, and then roll its payment into paying off the next property's mortgage when the first property is paid off.

Business Strategy

EACH OF YOU SHOULD USE WHATEVER GIFT YOU HAVE RECEIVED TO SERVE OTHERS, AS FAITHFUL STEWARDS OF GOD'S GRACE IN ITS VARIOUS FORMS.

—1 Peter 4:10

Why Get into Business?

You may never have thought of it this way, but when motivated by the right spirit and focus, a business is a form of service. For you to have the best experience and success as a business owner, maintaining the mind-set of a servant and instilling that into the culture of your business will ensure that your decision making is aligned with the people who ultimately pay your bills: your customers.

If you are considering starting a new business or taking over an existing one, I commend you for your vision. Business ownership is a great way to build a wealth legacy—but it is also a great way to lose one. So it is important that you go into the endeavor with realistic expectations and a proper understanding of why you are doing the particular business you have chosen.

Usually, your motivation for going into business is one or more of the five *P*s:

- *Passion.* You are especially passionate about a particular issue, and you envision that running a business where you get to be around your passion all day is your ideal life. For example, somebody who is always working out and around gyms decides that he or she wants to own a gym because he or she is passionate about fitness.

- *Personal skill.* You are especially good at a particular skill, and you believe people would be willing to pay you a premium for your services. An example of this is somebody who is a graphic designer for an advertising agency and decides to become a freelancer and get his or her own gigs because he or she wants more freedom and feels as if he or she would make more money overall.

- *Product or service.* You have an idea for a product or service that you believe has a market, and you want to build a business around it. This is often the type of motivation that serial inventors have for wanting to start a business.

- *Profit.* You want to create value in the marketplace that will translate into profit. People with this type of motivation are not necessarily tied to one particular area or topic but are constantly looking for underserved markets and trying to figure out how they can create a business model that would profitably reach the market—and ultimately increase their wealth.

- *Philosophy.* You want to change the world in a particular way through your business. This doesn't necessarily mean that the business is a nonprofit, but it does mean that there is an overarching cause or movement behind your motivation to start and run the business. An example of this type of philosophy-driven approach is a company such as Google, which has a very strong philosophy around making the world's knowledge accessible to as many people as possible.

Do you see in yourself any of these five motivations? If not, ask yourself why you really want to start the business, because I believe the most successful businesses have some degree of all five components that motivate them. Even if the business isn't a large corporation such as Google, you can still see a thread of these elements in a business that is being driven by the right motivations. For example, I have a financial-advising business, which I started after years of working for a financial corporation as a financial advisor. Here's how the five *Ps* fit with my business:

- *Passion.* I am writing a book about finances, so it is clear that this is an area of passion for me.
- *Personal skill.* I did very well as a financial advisor when I worked for a corporation, so I knew that I could take those same skills and use them as the foundation for starting my own practice.
- *Product or service.* I knew that I was very good at providing service to my clients, and this would translate well into the financial-advisor world, which is very relationship driven.
- *Profit.* I understood certain segments of the financial-advising market especially well and knew that I could communicate about finances to clients in a way that others couldn't, thus creating value in an underserved market.
- *Philosophy.* I hope that by reading this book, you can see that I have a very strong philosophy about the right way to build a financial legacy. This underlying philosophy is what drives the decisions that we make daily in my business.

So after you finish this exercise of understanding your motivations for starting or running a business, you will find more clarity as you make decisions about which products or services to provide and which markets to serve. This clarity is important because successful businesses are also focused businesses. You cannot be all things to all people, and therefore if you understand your business identity at a deep level, the next sections about how to make sure your business stays on track will flow naturally from your motivation.

The Business Dashboard

If you are running a business currently, or plan to run one very soon, you must develop a business dashboard to help you keep track of the health of your business. This will allow you to plan ahead of time for adjustments you need to make rather than reacting to what appear to be surprises. It will also help you to develop a repeatable system for success because you will know the key things that help your business succeed. Knowing those key things makes it much easier to focus your and your employee's efforts on the things that matter, even as your business grows and becomes more complex.

For example, if you are in sales or real estate, it might be important to track how many appointments you schedule every week, whereas if you have an online business, the number of appointments would not be a useful metric but the number of unique visitors you get on your website every day would. Every business has its own patterns and flows, so there is no one-size-fits-all approach to this kind of dashboard.

The best way to create a unique dashboard for your business is to understand the four basic business-metric groups and the seven stages of business growth. Knowing these concepts will help you determine what to measure and what types of benchmarks you should be measuring against.

Each of the sections I cover in the four business-metric groups should be represented by one or more numbers in your business dashboard, and the seven stages of business growth tell you where you need to focus within those metric groups based on what part of the business lifecycle you are experiencing. Even if you start out using a spreadsheet to cover these areas and monitor them, it is better than not measuring anything. So read the next two sections, and decide how you will customize them for your business.

The Four Business-Metric Groups

The four business-metric groups are based on the key areas that need to be on point in order for a business to be successful. You need to ensure that you have a very tight understanding of these four areas at all times with your business if you want it to be healthy:

- Excellent marketing
- Strong operations
- New products and services
- Money-metrics balance sheet

The first item, excellent marketing, is the lifeblood of your business because without customers all you have is a hobby at best. Marketing is simply the ways you let people know about your product or service so they are persuaded to find out more and buy. To be excellent at marketing, you need to know who your target customers are and the best ways to reach them. The answer to those two questions is very specific to the type of business that you do. For example, in my financial-advising business, one of our key forms of marketing is educational seminars because we know that people who are looking to learn more about how to manage their finances are likely to want some assistance in doing so. A seminar would be a horrible choice for marketing if I had a catering business though, because people don't want to sit down and learn about how I make my pies; they just want to eat them. A website, brochures, and free samples would be a much better form of marketing for that type of business.

The second area, strong operations, is how you deliver on the promises that you make through your marketing. Every business needs to have systems in place that ensure that you can deliver the same level of product and service repeatedly, and this is how you develop strong operations.

Some of the key areas that you should develop operational systems for are detailed in Michael Gerber's business classic *The E-Myth*. In that book he talks about three kinds of systems: hard, soft, and information. Hard systems are physical things that you put in place to do some of the components of your business that are repetitive or time consuming. An example of a hard system is something as simple as a brochure, which takes the place of you or one of your employees taking the time to pre-educate your clients about what you do and how you do it. Instead, the clients read the brochure by themselves and decide whether to call you. You may have to fill in some gaps when you finally talk, but it will be less time consuming. A website can serve this same purpose.

Soft systems are your people systems—the methods and practices you put in place to help each person on your team know what his or her job is and how best to execute it. You can capture your soft systems in clear job descriptions and operational manuals that describe the expected activities and behavior in each role.

Information systems are not the same thing as information technology (IT). Your information systems are the way you gather data about your business so that you can measure things and analyze how you are doing. The more accurate and timely this data is, the better informed your strategic decisions will be.

Once you ensure that your operations are tight, it's important to consistently develop new products and services. Some companies are really good at this, such as McDonald's and Apple, who have a new product available every year (sometimes even multiple times in a year). McDonald's started out with hamburgers, then added shakes, then added drive-through service, then started supersizing, and so on. Apple either builds on an existing product, as with all the different generations of the iPod it created, or creates a whole new category, as when it released the first iPhone and then the first iPad. What these companies have realized is that new products and services serve two purposes to keep a business healthy. First, they keep current customers engaged and excited about the business, which makes it more likely that customers will be loyal. And second, they attract new segments of the population that may not have been served in the past, which helps the business to continue growing.

The fourth business-metric group, what I call the money-metrics balance sheet, is the skeleton that holds the first three areas together. If the finances of your business have issues, there will be issues in your marketing, operations, and capability to release new products and services. The way the money behaves can tell you a lot about the overall health of your business and is a strong input into your overall decision making.

Put very simply, there are two key components of your business finances that you should always understand very well: your revenue and expenses. You must know what happens to every single dollar that flows through your business, and you must track this on a weekly basis. In addition to revenue and expenses, you need to understand your balance sheet as an overall measure of how much wealth is captured in your business. Your balance sheet compares how much you have to how much you owe; it is like the measurement you do to determine your personal net worth. For a business, the balance sheet is one of the key ways to learn whether it is a good idea to make a major investment in your business. It is also the way investors and potential partners will judge the riskiness of joining forces with you, so if you intend to grow your business significantly, it is important to keep this area healthy.

The four metric groups combine to provide a framework that you can develop to have a deep insight into your business on a weekly, monthly, quarterly, and annual basis. The image below shows you how all these areas fit together and what measurements to use for each area. The arrows on the left indicate the direction that you want each of the areas to be trending in order to have a healthy business.

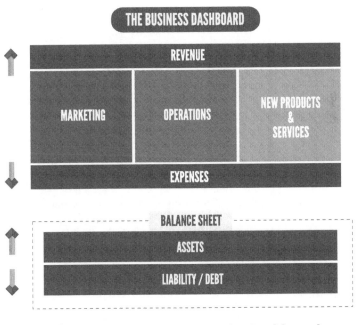

Figure 10: Your Business Metrics Dashboard

Now that you know the four major metric groups that your business dashboard should contain, you can figure out how to customize the dashboard for your particular business by understanding what stage of business growth you are in. In all stages, it is important to measure all the areas, but the kinds of things you should focus on differ based on where you are.

The Seven Stages of Business Growth

The seven stages of business growth help you to identify where you are in the growth cycle of your business. Just like human beings, businesses need to go through a process of growth, and as they pass through each stage, the things they focus on become different. This is similar to how your parenting has to evolve over time if you have children. When your children are newborns, you try to figure out what their crying means, and most of what you do is guesswork because they have only one way of providing you with feedback. As they develop into toddlers and begin speaking, they can actually tell you what they need in clearer terms, and you can respond accordingly. As they grow into their teen years, you have to further develop your communication style because you want them to learn how to make decisions for themselves—so instead of dictating what they do because you are the parent, you give them more input into their own path. Then when they develop into adults, your relationship with them evolves again; you become a sounding board for their plans while allowing them to become the controllers of their own destiny.

The first stage of business, the *seed stage*, is similar to the conception stage of a child's life, when it is still in the womb and is totally dependent on its mother for everything from oxygen to nutrition. In the seed stage, your business is an idea that has not come into the world yet; you are saving up your seed money to support it in its early days. This is the phase where you should develop clear plans about how you want to launch and how you will go after your first key customers. You need to give it enough time in the womb to get strong enough to start fending for itself when introduced into the world.

Your business dashboard in the seed stage is very simple—a list of all the potential leads for your first set of customers and how you plan to get them to buy your product or service. You may be tracking some expenses, but there is no revenue yet, and you haven't really set up operations. So your business-metric groups would look something like this:

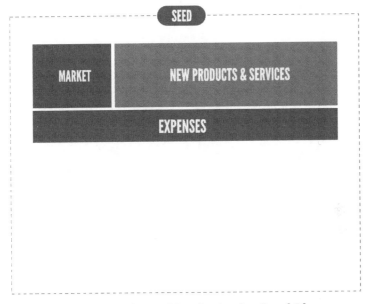

Figure 11: Business Metrics in the Seed Phase

The second stage is called the *start-up stage*. This is when you first open up for business. For example, if you are a food business, in the seed stage you were making pies for your friends and family, who were telling you that the pies were good enough to sell; now as a start-up, you start taking individual orders and charging people for the pies. You are very much in a hustle mode in this phase and should be focused on building up a predictable source of customers for your product or service.

Your business dashboard at this stage will be heavily focused on measuring your marketing activities and their effectiveness because you are focused on building up a customer base that you can rely on for steady revenue. You are most likely not profitable yet, so you are still investing in expenses for the business because your revenue will not cover all of them. Strong metrics to control your expenses are important at this stage, and you should start investing in creating your operating systems. Your business-metric groups would look something like this:

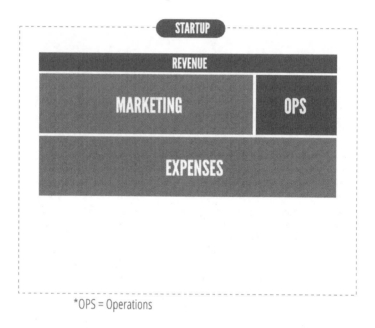

*OPS = Operations

Figure 12: Business Metrics in the Start-Up Phase

After the start-up phase, your next stage is *growth*. In our example with the pie business, you are transitioning from taking individual orders of pies to catering for events. And as you do more catering, you can no longer cook in your home kitchen and need to move to a commercial kitchen and get a truck to deliver your orders instead of your personal car.

In the growth phase, your revenue starts to take off, and you are taking on bigger one-time expenses to keep up with the revenue growth. You also start to introduce some new products and services as you identify larger segments that you can serve.

The dashboard for this period of your growth has to offer a very close look at expenses as a percentage of revenue because although investments to grow are required, it's important to make sure that they do not hurt the profitability of the company. You need to have a very clear budget for running the business that feeds into the metrics that you are tracking to make sure you are keeping within what you planned.

You should also have some clear marketing and operational statistics to track at this stage, and they should feature prominently on your dashboard. You should be able to see the effect of different marketing campaigns on your income versus their cost. And you should know what the costliest parts of your operation are and create a plan to minimize those expenses. Paying off debt should be a critical focus at this point.

Your dashboard would look like this:

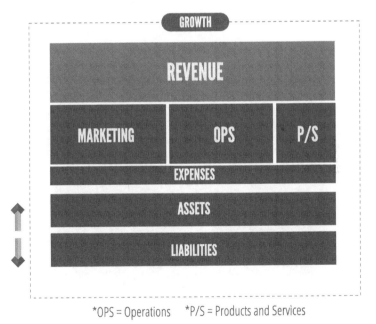

*OPS = Operations   *P/S = Products and Services

Figure 13: Business Metrics in the Growth Phase

After growth, you move into the *established stage.* In our catering example, this would be when you move from just doing catering to opening up a restaurant and having a physical location for your business. You are able to do this because you have a trusted way of forecasting your income and you have a tight control on your expenses, so you can anticipate what a big change such as this will do to the business's success.

In the established phase, you have an even split of focus on marketing, operations, and new products and services. Your business is in the zone, and everything is clicking, so your dashboard is focused mostly on making sure nothing falls through the cracks, as well as planning for opportunities that could get you into the next phase.

Your business dashboard is well developed and trustworthy at this point, and your whole company runs based on the metrics you track on the dashboard. Your employees and partners understand what needs to be done just as well as you do.

Your dashboard would look something like this:

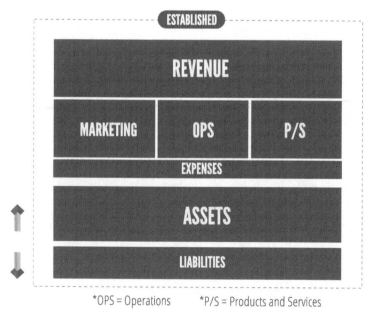

Figure 14: Business Metrics in the Established Phase

Once you have become established, your next move is into *expansion*. For some businesses, this may not be something that they are interested in doing, and they are fine staying in the established phase. For other business owners who are more ambitious, this is when you look for opportunities to make "leap" growth in your business. An example of this would be for a restaurant to open up multiple locations. Or if you were a media company that focused on a profitable podcast, you might decide to grow a video channel on YouTube.

For a brick-and-mortar type of business, this is the stage where you would get financing from banks and other investors because you need significant capital infusion into the business. You might even be looking at friends and fools (I mean friends and family) as investors.

In addition to the things you track as an established business, your dashboard needs to take a close look at your balance sheet because you are likely either using up some significant assets or taking on debt in order to support expansion.

The dashboard would look like this:

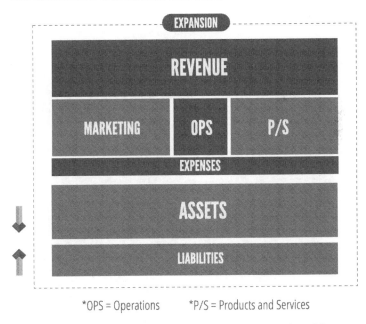

*OPS = Operations   *P/S = Products and Services

Figure 15: Business Metrics in the Expansion Phase

After expansion comes *maturity*. This is the phase where you have tapped into the major growth areas of your business and are reaping the benefits of steadily growing assets and revenue. Some businesses run for years at this stage and become a fixture in the community or in their broader market. They become the go-to brand for their particular brand or service. It is very important not to become complacent in this stage, because you still need to focus on creating new products and services to keep your target market engaged. If you don't continue evolving, the mature business will begin to shrink—or new competitors will come into the market and force your business to either change or die.

A business in the mature stage should also develop a succession plan because the leadership currently in place will not always be the same. There should be a clear view into the future, and you should identify people that can take over the mantle of leading the business, while keeping with its original vision and values, so that the business is a legacy business and not a one-hit wonder.

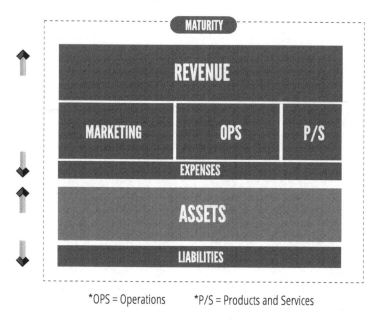

*OPS = Operations   *P/S = Products and Services

Figure 16: Business Metrics in the Maturity Phase

For some businesses, there is an additional stage after maturity called *exit*. Sometimes the sole purpose of growing a business is to eventually sell it off to investors—either publicly or privately. The exit can take many forms, including a private asset or stock sale, an acquisition or merger, or an initial public offering (IPO), where the company goes public. In each of the cases, you are transferring ownership of the business to another party.

Now that you understand the stages of business growth, it is important to understand that entrepreneurship is inherently unpredictable, so if things don't go exactly according to your business plan (and they most likely won't), you have to be flexible enough to react and make the necessary changes to survive. Business building is not for the fainthearted, and you have to be in it for the long run if you want to be successful. To manage your expectations for how long it might take to build your business, take a look at this illustration of the average timelines for each stage.

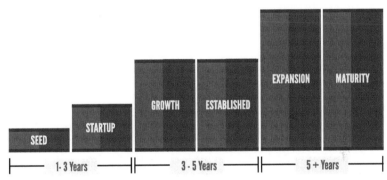

Figure 17: Timelines by Business Phase

As you can see, at a minimum you are making a three- to five-year commitment when you decide to go into business. So make sure you are very sure about the industry you have chosen and the product or service you will provide. You will need to invest time, sweat, tears, and money to make it work. If you are willing to do so, the rewards are tremendous and will make up a large chunk of your wealth-building portfolio.

Chapter 9: **Your Marriage and Your Money**

"HAVEN'T YOU READ," HE REPLIED, "THAT AT THE BEGINNING THE CREATOR 'MADE THEM MALE AND FEMALE,' AND SAID, 'FOR THIS REASON A MAN WILL LEAVE HIS FATHER AND MOTHER AND BE UNITED TO HIS WIFE, AND THE TWO WILL BECOME ONE FLESH'? SO THEY ARE NO LONGER TWO, BUT ONE FLESH. THEREFORE WHAT GOD HAS JOINED TOGETHER, LET NO ONE SEPARATE."

—Matthew 19:4–6 (NIV)

THERE IS NOTHING NOBLER OR MORE ADMIRABLE THAN WHEN TWO PEOPLE WHO SEE EYE TO EYE KEEP HOUSE AS MAN AND WIFE, CONFOUNDING THEIR ENEMIES AND DELIGHTING THEIR FRIENDS.

—Homer

I f you spend even a few minutes on the Internet reading about marriage and divorce, you will undoubtedly come across the statistic that 50 percent of marriages end in divorce. This statistic was based on studies about a cultural trend that happened in the late 1960s and into the 1970s but is not an accurate reflection of modern reality. Several articles, including one in the *New York Times*, have been written about how even though this statistic is incorrect, it does not seem to go away but persists as an urban myth.[11] In reality, the divorce rate has stabilized at a lower rate than the 50 percent that was quoted and is not on the rise. The success of your marriage is less in danger because of a cultural trend than it is because of actions and attitudes that you have complete control over.

Similar to success with finances, success in your marriage is driven by the principles that you and your spouse live by, and if these principles are grounded in wisdom, you have a great chance of fulfilling your vows "till death do you part." With that out of the way, let's focus on some of the positive things about marriage, especially with regard to your finances.

I have done a lot of marriage counseling over the last twenty years, and finances is one of the two most common areas that cause stress in those relationships. The second most common area is communication, and not surprisingly, the two interplay with each other. If your finances are in good order, typically your communication is better; talking to your mate while sitting on a beach in Jamaica and relaxing is much more pleasant than sitting at the kitchen table sorting through bills. Finance is one of the difficult topics for discussion in many relationships because there is so much emotion tied to what money means to each person. For one spouse, money might mean freedom, whereas to the other spouse, it means security. Each of these views about money might lead to very different priorities—some of which conflict in terms of what to practically do about the household finances. If the cou-

---

[11] "The Divorce Surge Is Over but the Myth Lives On," http://www.nytimes.com/2014/12/02/upshot/the-divorce-surge-is-over-but-the-myth-lives-on.html

ple's communication skills are poor, instead of the couple trying to better understand each other's point of view and find a place of compromise, the money conversations continuously lead to conflict or no money conversations happen at all, and each person builds up internal resentment for the other one because they are not in agreement.

Over the years, one of the things I have enjoyed doing is interviewing older couples that have been married for thirty years or longer. Those conversations have revealed to me three common themes that led to the success of their marriages. I think these themes are also important for couples to have success with their finances.

Three Principles of Successful Marriages

To understand what is special about couples that have been successfully married for thirty years or longer, I often interview them, and over the years, I have distilled their wisdom into three key principles.

#1: They Are Best Friends

In couples that have longevity, both people consider their spouse their best friend. They are able to get along beautifully with each other and enjoy spending time together. Generally, these couples have invested time in the relationship to grow closer to each other over the years and miss each other when they are apart. This friendship is especially important because things are not always romantic in a marriage, so when either person is less than his or her best, he or she knows that the relationship is still a safe space.

#2: They Know Each Other Really Well

The second theme is related to the first but is not exactly the same thing. In addition to being best friends, couples that have longevity know the details about who they each are—and accept it. They do not try to force the other person to be somebody he or she is not, and they make an effort to love the person based on who he or she is.

For example, I know that my wife likes to be around family on the holidays, so I always make sure that during that time our activities are centered on making time to be with them. I will go out of my way to make sure that family events take place at this time, and I actively participate in them. On the other hand, my wife knows that if I am driving to a speaking engagement or similar event, I like it to be completely silent in the car so that I can concentrate and focus on what I am going to do. So if she is riding with me to one of those events, she makes sure to give me that space without making a big deal about it.

#3: They Don't Go to Bed Angry

The principle of not going to bed angry doesn't mean that there aren't a few times when they go to bed angry at each other. The spirit of the rule is that the couple should be committed to resolving issues when they arise. Rather than fighting, staying mad because neither one of you is satisfied with the outcome, and letting that anger fester overnight—or over several days—they both understand the importance of peace in the marriage over being right. Sometimes the reason we stay in a place of conflict has more to do with pride than it does with truly finding a solution that serves both people. When a couple is mature enough to recognize that, fighting becomes more like intense fellowship than an MMA fight.

Ten Components of a *Financially* Successful Marriage

To be successful in marriage and also win financially, some components of the way you work together with money are critical. Personal finance when you are single involves only one decision maker; once you decide to do something with your money, you are the final authority and can move forward with your plans. By contrast, marriage is a partnership, so making decisions unilaterally and operating without the agreement of your partner is a form of manipulation and can lead to real emotional-abuse problems in the relationship. To ensure that you operate in unity when it comes to your money, I want to share ten things that I have seen that have helped couples succeed in their family finances.

#1: Mine, Yours, Ours, or HIS

When you first join together with somebody else in marriage, you have usually spent years operating as an individual. "Mine" is the way you think about your possessions and your money: it's "my" furniture, "my" apartment, "my" bank accounts, and so on. You are used to distributing your income solely to the affairs of your own household and your own needs.

When you are dating your future spouse, you think about his or her stuff as "your" furniture, "your" apartment, and "your" bank accounts. In fact, if he or she has student loans or credit cards, it's "your" debt as well. Though you may care about the person and help him or her out with individual situations, you still don't have a mind-set of ownership over his or her possessions and money, because you are not yet a combined household.

A critical mind-set shift that has to happen very quickly after getting married is recognizing that all the "mines" and "yours" have turned into "ours." Because you are one under God's eyes, you are now sharing all your possessions and money. Many couples struggle with this concept because they are missing one critical point of understanding about their possessions and money. They never realized that they didn't actually own any of the stuff all along; it has always belonged to God, and they are merely stewards.

When you understand that everything you have is actually not yours but God's and that you are a steward of those possessions, then the change from "mine" to "ours" is a situation where you are not losing (or gaining) anything. It is more like you are coming together to be co-managers of property that still belongs to the same owner.

With the mind-set of co-stewardship, your focus becomes doing what God wants you to do with the combination of your possessions and money instead of fighting about who gets to keep what and how things should be split up between you. This mind-set helps tremendously with the second attribute of couples that are successful financially, because it is driven by their desire to please God.

#2: Giving Is a Priority

> GIVE, AND IT WILL BE GIVEN TO YOU. A GOOD MEASURE,
> PRESSED DOWN, SHAKEN TOGETHER AND RUNNING OVER,
> WILL BE POURED INTO YOUR LAP. FOR WITH THE MEASURE
> YOU USE, IT WILL BE MEASURED TO YOU.
> —Luke 6:38 (NIV)

If a couple does not agree about how they will give as a part of their stewardship, they are setting themselves up for a long-standing conflict that will be impossible to resolve. Though the easiest place to deal with this is in the household finances and tithing, this idea of giving extends to other areas of giving that make up their stewardship: their time and their talents. And it is not only about giving to the church.

When thinking about giving time, how much time do you spend with your spouse? Do you intentionally sacrifice things that you would like to spend your time doing so you can do something that your spouse wants to do? Do you organize your schedule so that your spouse is a priority?

And with your talent, do you use your God-given talents to be a blessing to your spouse? If you have a writing gift, do you write your spouse poems and letters? If you are a great singer, do you sing to your spouse and give your spouse "personal concerts"? Or in a more practical manner, do you have a gift of administration? Are you great at organizing things? How do you use that gift to make your spouse's life better (without trying to force your spouse to be as organized as you)? You can be as creative as you want in this area since it is really based on your gifts.

Finally, back on the topic of money—or your "treasure"—if you looked at your last ten transactions in your bank account, what would they say about where your heart is? Is your spending in line with loving your spouse, or does it tell a different story? Make sure that the evidence supports the story you are telling yourself.

#3: Operate on a Family Budget

To make your stewardship practical, you need to turn it into a written plan. When it comes to finances, that written plan is your budget. And when you are married, the budgeting process cannot be done in isolation, because you are now in co-stewardship of your money.

Whenever I begin teaching on this topic, the question about separate versus joint bank accounts comes up. Some people believe that each spouse should have his or her own account where-as others believe that everything should be in a joint account. I generally suggest one of two ways of doing this. One way is for the two spouses to each have individual accounts and then share one joint account. That is how about 90 percent of the couples I work with have things set up. The other way is to have all accounts jointly held; this generally happens when two people get married really young, before they have a significant financial footprint, or with older couples over fifty-five, who have simplified finances and manage everything together. I used to teach that you should always combine everything, as in the second option, but I have become a little more flexible on this issue. Both approaches work as long as there is transparency between the two of you, and the account that all the household bills are paid out of is a joint account and managed centrally.

In terms of creating the budget, I usually illustrate three approaches. The first is a straightforward, normalized budget that covers all of the major spending categories. The second is the before-you-retire budget that you use to compare how you are spending currently to how you will be spending when you retire and potentially have income that has to be more tightly managed. The third is a very detailed budget that I use with our Total Wealth Management program when you want to do a very close tracking of your spending on a monthly basis to find opportunities for improving your financial situation. You can find samples of these three at http://www.yourwealthcycle.com/budget.

Whichever one of the three budgets you work with, it's important to make sure that you continuously review it together and use it as a tool to guide your family conversations about money. Don't just create a pretty, well-formatted document and then file it away without using it in your real life.

#4: Have Team Goals

AND THE LORD ANSWERED ME, AND SAID, WRITE THE VISION, AND
MAKE IT PLAIN UPON TABLETS, THAT HE MAY RUN THAT READETH IT.
—Habakkuk 2:2

The fourth attribute that helps to drive your financial success as a couple is to have team goals. In Habakkuk, God talks about writing the vision and making it plain upon tablets, meaning that you want to have your vision for your life together written out big and bold so that you can both see it clearly. People who don't write down their goals have a very low chance of achieving them. And if you want to operate in unity as a couple, it's important to use your written goals to make sure that the two of you are moving in the same direction rather than striving for different and sometimes opposite things. Also, a large number of your family goals have a financial component to them, so operating on them as a team increases your success financially.

The first thing to get clear on as a couple is the difference between a need, a want, and a wish. Create a scale from one through ten that you use to rank things, with ten meaning it is something that is nonnegotiable and has to happen, and one meaning that it is purely a wish. Everything you discuss in your goals should fall within this scale.

For the items that get a ten, remember Philippians 4:13, which reads: "And my God will meet all your needs according to the riches of his glory in Christ Jesus." That means that everything belongs to God and God provides all your needs, so you have to trust Him to provide for you if you are holding up your end of the deal. Note, though, that it does not say "greed," so make sure that the needs you write down are truly things that you cannot do without—rather than things that you just really want.

So what are some examples of needs? One thing that falls out-side of your scale and should come first before everything is your tithe, but if you have been paying attention so far, you already know that. So number one after giving is housing; your mortgage or rent has to be paid. This should get a ranking of ten. Next, at number nine, are your bills, such as electricity, gas, and water. These all fall in the realm of needs.

Wants are things like travel. Whether the ranking for travel is a seven or a four depends on how important it is to you as a couple ver-sus other wants. For couples that love to travel, this would be a highly ranked want that may come before things such as driving a luxury car or going out to eat every week. Other couples may rank travel lower and focus their wants on eating out and driving the latest cars.

A wish is a want that requires significant planning. For exam-ple, a wish may be to pay for your daughter's wedding or take your family on a trip through Europe. These items are on the list of your goals, and you strive for them with the understanding that to achieve them requires a process and discipline if you want to pay for them the right way. Home renovations, wealth building, and retirement accounts fall into this category.

#5: Agree on Timelines

In addition to having joint financial goals as a couple, it is import-ant to agree on shared timelines that you are both planning the future against. The best way to categorize your goal timelines is as short term, medium term, and long term. I recommend that you discuss what you would like to accomplish financially in the next eighteen months as the short term, two to five years as the medium term, and six-plus years as the long term. The reason I use two to five years is that medium-term goals can be accelerated depending on what you are willing to sacrifice. If you want to buy a house and are saving $100 per month, it might take you a while. But if you increase that amount to $500 per month, it can happen much quicker, and you can begin shortening those timelines.

If you know your goals and your timelines, then you are most of the way toward successful financial planning as a couple. There are some specific plans that are very important to work on together as a couple. Those compose the next set of attributes for financial success together.

#6: Do GOOD Together

If you have forgotten from earlier in the book, GOOD stands for "get out of debt," and you can refer to the illustrations earlier in the book on this topic. The important point I want to highlight here is that it is critical for you as a couple to have a get-out-of-debt plan that acknowledges that there is no such thing as "my debt and your debt." If you are a married couple, your spouse's debt is your debt, and your debt is your spouse's debt. In other words, if your spouse owes $20,000, he or she doesn't have that loan by himself or herself; you both have a $20,000 loan.

Proverbs 22:7 says, "The rich rule over the poor, and the borrower is servant to the lender." So you can't think you are free if your spouse is imprisoned in debt; you both have to get out together because you are one in God's eyes.

#7: Family Wealth-Building Plan

Along with your debt plan, it's important to have a family wealth-building plan. You may be familiar with the story in Matthew 25:14–30, where a wealthy man goes on a journey and entrusts his three servants with money to take care of until he returns. The Bible says he gave each of them talents, which are portions of gold; one talent would be the equivalent of over $600,000 at today's gold prices. So the servant who was given one talent had $600,000, the one with two talents had $1.2 million, and the one with five talents had $3 million. These were not small amounts to be entrusted with, but the principles of the story are the same regardless of how much money you have in surplus. In the story, the first servant with the least amount of money was so worried about losing the money that he did nothing with it—he did the equivalent of hiding it under his mattress until his master returned. The other two invested the money and made it grow. When the master returned, he applauded the two who invested the money and chastised the one who did nothing with it—in fact, he took the money away from him and gave it to the servant who had gotten the best return with his money. You cannot do what the first servant did and bury your money or put it under your mattress; you need to find a way to make it grow through a wealth-building plan.

There should be at least four elements to that wealth-building plan: long-term investing, real estate, asset protection, and tax management. For most people, who do not have a lot of investable assets, your long-term investing plan is primarily tied up in your retirement investments. So make sure that if you are both working, you both have a 401(k) if you work for a for-profit company, a 403(b) if you are working at a nonprofit company, a 457 if you work for a city, or at least an IRA, which is an individual retirement account, or an SEP (simplified employee pension). If any one of these is in place and you still have investable money, then make sure to have a brokerage account.

In addition to your long-term investing, you should have real estate in your wealth-building plan. If you are newly married without kids and are looking to purchase a house, instead of going the traditional route of a single-family home, buy a multifamily home with two, three, or four units so that you can create income through the rentals. By doing so, you can maximize your income through that real estate investment and set yourself up better financially when you start having children and move to a single-family home. In fact, when you move to the single-family, you should keep the multifamily as your first investment property. You can then add on to this real estate investment portfolio over the years until you have a sizeable amount of income-producing properties in your wealth-building plan.

As you are accumulating all these assets, both in your investments and in real estate, it is very important to protect yourselves against loss by using insurance. Make sure you both understand all the different risks that you have to insure against, including health, death, disability, property damage, and liability. A good insurance agent will be able to help you determine what types of coverage make the most sense for you, but those are the five major categories.

You may also need to consider long-term care insurance if you have elderly parents who will need your care. The main reason to have insurance is that each of the risks you insure against has the potential to erode all of the hard work you have done in your wealth-building plan, and without it, you could lose years of investments just from one shock event.

#8: Estate Plan

> A GOOD PERSON LEAVES AN INHERITANCE FOR THEIR CHILDREN'S CHILDREN, BUT A SINNER'S WEALTH IS STORED UP FOR THE RIGHTEOUS.
>
> —Proverbs 13:22

According to Biblical wisdom, it is important to think about and plan for more than just your own generation. True financial success lives through several generations, so you have to think about your children and their children when organizing your finances. The practical way to do this is through your estate plan, so it is important that you both understand wills and trusts. The specifics of how you set these up are beyond the scope of this book, so make sure to meet with an estate planner and set up the appropriate structures for your specific situation. You have to ensure that you have a living trust, a durable power of attorney, and all your health-care directives in place. This is something that people in their twenties and thirties often don't think about, but if you are married, you have to be responsible to your spouse and discuss each of these documents and what they mean for your wishes when you die. We all plan to live long lives, but sometimes, that is not God's plan.

#9: Kids Plan

In my previous books about personal finance, I was not a parent, so this section is brand new to me. Now that I have three children, I strongly believe that you have to have a kids plan as part of your financial plan. Your first reaction when I say this might be to jump right to saving for college, but the kids plan starts even before that. There are some real kid costs that start right from when they are born that you have to factor into your plan—especially if your family is growing and you still plan to have more children.

I have two children in preschool and one in daycare, and their school costs alone are up to $1,000 a month. Even if your kids go to a free school or a charter school, there are still fundraisers and extracurricular activates that can get to be quite expensive when you add them all up. There was a little event at my kids' preschool where kids could learn to play either tennis or soccer or another sport. As a parent, you want your kids to be involved, so I was willing to pay the forty dollars for that. Since I have twins, this was close to a hundred dollars a month on just that activity. Then my sons are in karate, which is another fifty dollars times two (before the bill for sparring gear and their gi)—another hundred dollars per month minimum.

These investments are important because one of your most important responsibilities as a parent is to be a caretaker of your children's talents. So it is your responsibility to make sure that you provide opportunities for them to explore each of those areas that may be talents. To make sure that you do this in a disciplined way without blowing your overall financial plan, these types of costs must be in your budget and planned ahead for.

In addition to these preliminary costs, you should definitely be on top of planning for college costs very early in their childhood. Look at what college costs are right now, and then assume they will rise at 8 percent per year. Private institutions right now range from $50,000 to $60,000 per year, so if you have a five-year-old, it's going to cost about $90,000 per year for him or her to go to college. Make sure to start your children's college funds early.

#10: Create Financial Intimacy

The final element that makes everything go together financially as a couple is making sure that you and your spouse create something called financial intimacy. I know, when you think of the word "intimacy," money and budgeting are not the first things that come to mind, and it doesn't sound very exciting. But once you master this component, all the other nine become easier to do together as a team.

Your intimacy as a couple is affected by relationships with money because it is such an integral part of everybody's day-to-day life. To make sure that you grow together in your finances, you have to institute a safe space for the two of you to discuss financial matters on a weekly basis. The best way to start this off is to set aside some time where the two of you are alone, and use a blank piece of paper to list out each other's positive financial attributes. For example, my wife is very frugal, and I appreciate that about her. I can look at our bank account on Monday and leave town only to return on Thursday, and the bank account has exactly the same balance. I don't know whether I married her just to see how she managed to do this, but her frugality is something that caught my attention early on when we were dating. In our early days of courtship, I think on our third date, we were walking around the convention center after running a marathon, and she looked really cute, so I asked her whether she would like a bottle of water. She looked at me in disbelief and said, "Not at two twenty-five per bottle!" I think that's when I knew I would marry her.

There are other things that you could note about each other and your finances that are positive; that was just an example from my marriage. The key is to make sure you write out your appreciation for each other so you can start to identify where one of you is stronger than the other and might be better suited for one aspect of your financial lives. Remember, you are a team, and it shouldn't fall on one person to carry all the load.

Some things that tend to be gender specific that can help with financial intimacy are things such as a man understanding the importance of his wife feeling as though he adores her. Your actions with money should make her feel as if you are putting her on the top of your priority list. And for women, men need to feel as if they are respected, so find ways to acknowledge your husband's contributions and how important they are to the household.

For men, make sure to actually have a plan. One of a woman's greatest needs is security, and the less you have a vision of where things are going, the more insecure she will feel and therefore less likely to trust your actions. You might feel as if she is disrespecting you by asking so many questions all the time about what is happening with the money, but this might just be feedback that you don't have a solid plan or you have not communicated the plan well enough. Just tell her the plan. It's as simple as taking the lead and saying, "Hey, this is how I see us getting out of debt. This is where I see us going on vacation. This is how we are going to buy a house. This is the business I see us running in a few years."

Create a vision that is compelling and takes into account the desires of both your hearts, and then work together toward that vision as stewards. The vision you have been given as a couple is unique and special to you, and the way you handle your finances together will determine how well you realize that vision together—for yourselves, for your children, and for your legacy.

Chapter 10: **Money in the Bank**

I have two siblings—an older brother and a twin sister. When we were growing up, our father pushed us to be excellent in everything that we did. This was especially true in athletics where he added his own "home practice" to the practices we already had. For example, when we came home from basketball practice, he would make us take twenty-five free throws in a row before we could go inside for dinner. At the time we did not understand his methods and even thought he was a little crazy.

What usually happened is that my older brother would take his twenty-five shots and hit them easily. Then he'd wave good-bye and go inside while my sister and I continued attempting to reach twenty-five. Then my sister would usually complete her shots shortly after him, and I would be the last one attempting to complete the requirement. My sister was usually gracious enough to stay outside and act as my "encourager" as I continued my attempts.

I remember one night I was out there for a long time—it was a cold Minnesota night and it might have even been drizzling. I hit fifteen, sixteen, and seventeen, and then I missed. Then I'd get to twenty, twenty-one, twenty-two, and miss. At one point, I missed with about a couple of baskets away from twenty-five, and my dad threw the basketball back to me and started walking back into the house. So I thought to myself, "Great—he sees how much I've been trying and is gonna give me a break." So I followed him toward the house as he went into the garage. But just as he got to the end of the garage, he walked over to a switch and flipped on the outside lights. Then he turned back and walked me back to the basketball court and told me to keep shooting.

I was livid—and convinced that he was a maniac.

As he threw me the ball for each shot, he began exhorting me by saying things like, "I'm doing this so that you know how to make the shot under pressure. It doesn't matter whether you are cold or wet—you will still make the shot. I'm doing this so that you know how to get it done regardless of the situation. I'm doing this so you can win."

And we stayed out there until I hit my twenty-five shots.

I often think back on this story when I am teaching about the Jeremiah 29 scripture that talks about how God has a purpose for each of us. In that scripture there are two parts to the phrase: "I know the plans I have for you." The first part, "I know," refers to the knowledge God has about your situation. Regardless of what you are going through, He ultimately already knows what it is and even knows what comes after your current situation. The second part is that there is a plan for you—things are not just happening haphazardly.

When my dad had us outside shooting twenty-five free throws in a row, he was operating based on his knowledge of the game-time situations we were going to face in the future. Even if we could not see what he was doing—and were getting frustrated by it—ultimately it was for our own good.

The same is true with your financial life. Sometimes it may feel like you are facing a lot of challenges, and it is not clear why God is allowing them to happen. Instead of letting those situations discourage us, we can have peace in the understanding that He knows what He is doing—and why He is doing it. We just need to trust Him.

Our response in those situations should be based on the understanding of three things:

1. There is a plan.
2. You need to work the plan.
3. If you work the plan, you will win.

When you know that there is a plan, you become grounded and stop operating like a victim. You have clarity about your actions because you know that they will eventually lead to a better end. When my dad started yelling out to me his plan about the free throws, I stopped thinking he was crazy and realized everything he was doing was based on a greater wisdom that he was trying to instill in us. With that understanding, I changed my perspective.

From that point on, when we went out to shoot the free throws, instead of wondering when the torture would end, I just worked the plan—which is the second part of your response to God's plan for you. It required patience because at first I wasn't as good as my brother or sister and had to stay out longer than them—but I had to be consistent while trusting that my father saw a triumphant outcome at the end.

In your financial life, the concepts I have taught you in this book are your plan. Trust in the plan, and work the plan while understanding that the real fruit of your labor will take time. Things may not turn around quickly—but they will turn around eventually. Because the principles in this book are not based on my plan for you—they are based on God's plan for you as his steward. He not only wants you to tap into the fullness of the resources He has available for you, but He also wants to make sure that you are able to manage them well when you get them.

Going back to the example of basketball, there are certain players like Magic Johnson, Michael Jordan, and more recently LeBron James whom I refer to as "money in the bank." When everything is on the line and you need to get the ball to somebody who is going to give you the best chance to win, getting the ball in their hands is like "money in the bank" because there is a very high probability that they will get the job done and win the game. In the case of my experience as a twelve-year-old basketball player, the twenty-five free throws a night translated into a superior confidence on the court when it came to basketball season. I would proactively ask the coach to get the ball into my hands, and after taking the shot, I would yell out "Money!"—because I knew it was going in. I had worked the plan, and because I had worked the plan, I had confidence in my victory.

God wants you to get to the place where you have worked His plan so consistently that you have superior confidence in His plan and His power when it comes to your finances. Even when you cannot see the larger master plan for your life, you can always see the path you have to follow, because He has laid it out plainly for you to see. It is up to you whether or not you will walk on the path—you have the power to choose. He wants you to see every opportunity that He places before you as "money in the bank." He wants you to walk in the confidence of understanding that all you have to do is the work—and the victory will be yours.

This book has laid out that path for you. Choose to walk on it.

Made in the USA
San Bernardino, CA
20 January 2018